赵琛 著

中国建筑工业出版社
CHINA ARCHITECTURE & BUILDING PRESS

世界文化遗产　辽宁卷

昭陵

WORLD HERITAGE
LIAONING VOLUME
ZHAOLING IMPERIAL
TOMB

罗哲文收赵琛为入门弟子
Professor Luo Zhewen accepted Zhao Chen as his apprentice

序言——星星之火

我对关外"一宫三陵"非常了解,当年申遗时,我还提议,三陵不可分割,以扩展项目参与申遗,并一举成功。当前我国古建研究面临的现状,建筑专业很少开课,古建技术即将失传,那些既是艺术家又是工人的建筑研究者们,后继无人。古建筑是凝固的历史,一个没有历史的民族就好比一个人失去了记忆,我多么希望后辈学者能够接过先师与我手中的尺笔,好好保护祖国几千年遗留下来的那些古建筑遗产。

当年,赵琛拿着厚厚的一摞书稿,以"愿乞一言以托不朽"的谦虚与诚恳的态度邀我为他作序,我内心生出万千感慨,也产生了很重的责任感。而这次,是我第三次为他写序言了,写他家乡的遗产。赵琛以家乡人的角度去看世界文化遗产,当然比其他人更多一份了解,更多一份感情,也更多一份权威。他始终站在全局的角度,客观描述历史,尤其是对清代帝王陵寝学的研究,将整个清代陵寝作为一个体系,不孤立不分割,横向对比,纵向研究,可谓独树一帜。很多人都了解自己家乡,自己周围的事,却不能了解全局,赵琛恰恰能做到既了解家乡,又了解全局,"知己知彼"。清代陵寝的保护工作也没有做到这样,几乎陵与陵之间都是单独个体,甚至没有联系,没有整体意识,对文物的保护也是相当不利的。赵琛的这种思维,给我们一种思考,一种关于文化遗产保护的整体思考。关于中国的文物保护工作,不是各自顾各自,也不是一个人单打独斗能够完成的。

赵琛,一个人能够二十余年,锲而不舍,持之以恒地做一件事,可以说是很了不起的,尤其是古建筑研究并没有经济上的收入。只摄影一项,就需要大量的金钱投入,有人说:"想让谁破产,就送他照相机"。现在的时代,是金钱时代,一些年轻人赚来的钱,都用于享受生活了。没有钱的工作,没人愿意干。然而就算一个人有足够的资金,也未必有这样的时间和兴趣。据我了解,赵琛这个人没什么嗜好,赚来的钱都花在古建研究上和摄影上了。很多人不理解赵琛,然而我理解。可能是因为他是学美术的,所以对美学很有研究,因此在摄影上他比其他人更懂得审美和构图,加上他有胆识,有见识,更有猎人一样的耐力和精准的洞察力,使他在摄影上的造诣远非一般人能及。每次见到他,我的内心都会想到那句古话,所谓"天将降大任于斯人也"。

"德成而上,艺成而下",赵琛却可以说是德艺双馨了,出类拔萃,是同代学者中的佼佼者。七十年间,我研究古建筑,照片和摄影集看多了,只有文字的考察报告也看了很多,都觉枯燥,没什么新意。这本书却以独特的视觉,集摄影、绘画、文字于一体,摄影作品精彩,绘画生动真实,文字通俗易懂,三者结合,而治学态度严谨,书中甚至指出了申遗时测绘不准确的地方。曹雪芹写红楼,十年辛苦不寻常,赵琛却用二十余年时间做古建研究,时间的累积,阅历的丰富,知识的广博,其著作的内容和水平,同类书籍实难比肩。此外,全书还蕴涵了深厚的民族情感,对古建研究的未来的担忧,对历史文化传承的发扬,对后来人的培养与关注。作者始终站在历史的角度,纵观全局,将自己的渺小融于热爱的古建研究中去,不拘泥于个人,不局限于时代,体现出一种无私的大爱与博爱。再次为赵琛作序,我深觉缘分匪浅,他以一己之力,力撑古建这座欲将倾颓之厦,使我在耄耋之年,总算看到了一点希望,"星星之火,期以燎原",同时也对他在学术上有如此硕果而深表祝贺。

PREFACE — SPARKS OF FIRE

When Professor Zhao Chen invited me with an unpretentious sincerity to draw up a preface for his newly crafted manuscript under the pretext of "soliciting a word for the honor of eternity," my heart was overcome with strong emotions, sensing a heavy burden of responsibility as well. This is my third time to write a preface for his works on legacies of his hometown.

I know quite well about "the Imperial Palace and Three Imperial Mausoleums" outside Shanhai Pass. I proposed then to combine the three mausoleums as an integral extended part in the application for World Heritage, and fortunately succeeded at one stroke. Currently, ancient Chinese architecture research is confronted with multifold problems, for instance, few ancient architecture courses are lectured, ancient architectural techniques are not being handed down and none is willing to inherit the craftsmanship of those architecture researchers who are both artists and architects. Ancient architecture is more or less like cemented and solidified history, and a nation without history is like a man with no memory. How I wish that the younger people could take over the historic task of preserving the legacy of our ancient architecture handed down through thousands of years. Professor Zhao Chen examines the world heritage from a perspective of a local scholar, which helps ensure a better understanding with a touch of emotion and a tinge of authority. He always stands on a global position so that he can see the panorama clearly and describe history objectively. He has done a spectacular job in his study of imperial mausoleums of Qing Dynasty, at which he looks as an integral system with methods of horizontal contrast and longitudinal researches. Many people know about their hometown and things around, but few understand things as a whole. However, Zhao Chen is one of the few who boast of holoscopic insights regarding mausoleums both in hometown and throughout China. The protection of Qing mausoleums faces a dilemma, i.e. each mausoleum is protected separately without due consideration of preserving them as a whole, which is undoubtedly detrimental to heritage protection. What Zhao Chen has done ignites the introspection concerning the conundrum of how to carry out the nationwide cultural heritage preservation and protection, for a sound solution can't be guaranteed by relying merely on individual or separate efforts.

Professor Zhao Chen can be crowned with the wreath of greatness for his more-than-twenty-years unremitting perseverance in his study of ancient architecture, and, in particular, for the fact that it brings no economic returns. Take photography for example, it consumes a large amount of money, and a saying goes like this, "If you want someone to go bankrupt, send him a camera." In an era of hot materialist pursuit when some young people dissipate their earnings, no job can arouse much attention or attraction if it brings no money at all. Even a person who is well off may have no time or think it uninteresting to study ancient architecture. As far as I know, Zhao Chen is attached to nothing but ancient architecture study and photography, in which he spends extravagantly. Many people probably don't understand why, but I can understand his devotion. He majored in art with deep understanding of aesthetics, so he knows better the beauty and composition of photography. In addition, with his courage and knowledge, single-minded stamina, and accurate insights, he has made great achievements in photography that common people couldn't match. Every time I lay my eyes on him, a saying naturally jumps out into my mind, "God is about to place great responsibilities on this man."

"The achievement in virtue is held to be of superior worth, and the accomplishment of art in the next place." Professor Zhao Chen, one of the top scholars, can be acclaimed to be eximious in his quest of both virtue and art. In the course of ancient architecture study for the last seventy years, I have seen plenty of photos and albums and read a good many of tedious plain reports, most of which are humdrum and boring. But this book has a unique vision presented through combining photography, drawing and text. Wonderful photography, vivid drawing, easy-to-understand text, plus Zhao's rigorous attitude in the study, all these features make the book outstanding. The minor mistake made in surveying and mapping in application for World Cultural Heritage well illustrates Zhao's preciseness with facts and figures. It took ten years of extraordinary hardship for Cao Xueqin to finish the classic Dream of Red Mansions, while the study of ancient architecture cost Zhao over twenty years of his life. The author's timeless efforts, rich experience, extensive knowledge, and unique content of the book make this book unparalleled. What's more, his strong patriotism, his love and anxiety for ancient architecture, his concerns over passing down and cultivating a love for historical and cultural heritage could be sensed between lines of this book. Zhao always takes a historical perspective and devotes himself to the study of ancient architecture without considering individual welfare or limitation of his time, which demonstrates his selflessness and broadmindedness. I do feel it a great honor, at my ripe age, to write a few words for Zhao's book again, and want here to extend my heart-felt congratulations on his academic achievements. His devotion and commitment to ancient Chinese architecture and culture kindles my hope in preserving and resurrecting ancient Chinese culture, believing "a little spark can start a prairie fire."

LUO Zhewen

目 录
CONTENTS

序言——星星之火
PREFACE—SPARKS OF FIRE

智者乐水 / 6
THE WISE TAKE PLEASURE IN RIVERS AND LAKES / 8

事死如生的陵寝学 / 10
STUDY OF MAUSOLEUM: HONORING THE DEAD AS THE LIVING / 10

哲学思想决定建筑风格 / 12
PHILOSOPHIC THINKING DETERMINES ARCHITECTURAL STYLE / 13

少见的火葬皇陵 / 14
UNUSUAL MAUSOLEUM WITH CREMATED EMPEROR / 14

昭陵是清朝兴衰的缩影 / 14
ZHAOLING IMPERIAL TOMB AS A MINIATURE OF THE RISE AND FALL OF QING DYNASTY / 14

皇帝至此下马 / 17
DISMOUNTING TABLET—THE SPOT WHERE EVEN EMPERORS NEED TO DISMOUNT / 18

来自华表的灵感 / 21
INSPIRING HUABIAO / 22

连接阴阳两界的神桥 / 24
SPIRIT BRIDGE, LINK BETWEEN LIFE AND DEATH / 27

无名牌坊 / 28
ANONYMOUS MEMORIAL ARCH / 33

罕见的水冲御厕 / 35
UNUSUAL IMPERIAL TOILET WITH FLUSHING SYSTEM / 36

正红门的学问 / 41
ENIGMA OF FRONT RED GATE / 42

来自龙壁的灵感 / 45
INSPIRATION FROM DRAGON WALL / 47

给灵魂走的神道 / 48
SPIRIT PATH / 50

东西红门 / 52
EAST AND WEST RED GATES / 54

石象生花纹数量之谜 / 57
RIDDLE OF NUMBER OF DECORATIVE PATTERN ON STONE ANIMAL STATUES / 60

不是所有清帝都能立神功圣德碑 / 67
GREAT STELE PAVILION OF DIVINE MERITS, NOT ERECTED FOR ALL EMPERORS / 68

昭陵祭祀 / 75
ZHAOLING IMPERIAL TOMB SACRIFICES / 76

清代帝陵独有的方城 / 79
SQUARE CITY, WHICH ONLY MAUSOLEUMS OF QING DYNASTY POSSESS / 80

倒插的隆恩门 / 82
EMINENT FAVOR GATE, WHICH CAN BE LATCHED FROM OUTSIDE / 84

摄影的最佳视点——角楼 / 94
TURRETS — IDEAL SPOT OF PHOTO-TAKING / 96

为太宗帝后灵魂居住的隆恩殿 / 99
HALL OF EMINENT FAVOR: RESTING PLACE FOR TAI TSU (EMPEROR HONG TAIJI) AND HIS EMPRESS / 105

皇孙膝下的拜石 / 110
WORSHIP STONE UNDER KNEES OF IMPERIAL DESCENDANTS / 113

皇太极与博尔济吉特氏的世代姻缘 / 114
MARRIAGES OF HONG TAIJI WITH BORJIGIT HALA / 115

皇太极最爱的牌位都无权进入东配殿 / 122
EAST SIDE-HALL, NOT FOR MEMORIAL TABLETS OF HONG TAIJI'S FAVORITE CONCUBINES / 124

皇帝生母的牌位也无权进入西配殿 / 126
WEST SIDE-HALL, NOT EVEN FOR MEMORIAL TABLET OF EMPEROR'S MOTHER / 128

被忽略的配楼 / 131
NEGLECTED SIDE PAVILION / 133

阴阳两界的邮局——焚帛亭 / 134
SILK-BURNING PAVILION — POST OFFICE BETWEEN LIFE AND DEATH / 136

人无路，魂有道的二柱门 / 139
DUAL PILLAR GATE — SPIRITS PATH OF THE DEAD RATHER THAN FOR THE LIVING / 140

不朽的供桌——石五供 / 142
LONGLASTING ALTAR — STONE FIVE OFFERINGS / 144

多灾多难大明楼 / 146
CALAMITOUS GRAND MING TOWER / 148

数理与昭陵风水 / 151
NUMBER AND ZHAOLING IMPERIAL TOMB FENGSHUI (GEOMANCY) / 152

清东陵被盗"逼走"溥仪 / 153
EXCAVATION OF EAST QING MAUSOLEUM, THE REASON WHY PU YI BECAME PUPPET EMPEROR / 154

月牙城还是哑巴院？/ 156
CRESCENT CITY OR DUMB COURTYARD ? / 156

神树与大清的命运 / 159
DIVINE TREE AND FATE OF GREAT QING DYNASTY / 159

宝顶的秘密 / 160
SECRETS OF BLESSED VAULT / 160

古松也是文物 / 162
AGED PINES ARE ALSO ANTIQUITY / 162

哪来的蛇神庙 / 164
MYSTERIES OF ZOMBIE TEMPLE / 164

结语——四十三年分之一秒 / 166
CONCLUSION— 1 SECOND V.S. 43 YEARS / 168

注解 / 172
NOTES / 173

智者乐水

第一次进昭陵时，我才3岁，是父母带我去的，现在已经记不太清了，即使拿着当时的照片，还是在脑海里搜寻不出什么记忆。

我想，我对昭陵的感情，更多的是缘于母亲。5岁那一次记忆就非常深刻，因为沈阳的学生每年春天都要到抗美援朝烈士陵园扫墓，扫墓之后要到北陵游玩，我便随母亲的同事同去。母亲的同事领我在方城的马道上绕了一周，站在高高的城墙上，看不见母亲，我心里很着急，便央求那位阿姨带我回去，找到母亲后，就开始吃午餐，结果却被那位阿姨笑话，说我不是要找母亲，是为了吃香肠、面包。其实，当时我是真的很害怕，对于那位阿姨并不熟悉，又看不见母亲，站在高墙上，向四周望去，只见一片黑幽幽的森林和满是身穿白衣服的孩子。越想越害怕，就更加着急见到母亲。因为被误解，才一直对这件小事耿耿于怀，对那次游昭陵的印象也特别深刻。

小时候，感觉昭陵的水无限大，一眼看不到边际，也总听人讲在昭陵的湖里淹死过人，这让年幼的我，在心理上对昭陵也感到害怕。十几岁的时候，我才绕昭陵里的一个湖走了一周，二十几岁时有了自行车，才骑车把所有的湖都绕了一圈，尤其是夏天，气温很高，但昭陵湖边上骑车的时候，明显感到背上有凉风抚过，有烟波致爽之感。昭陵湖边的温度，比市内要低几度。昭陵，就好比沈阳的"肺"，时时使人呼吸着清新凉爽的空气。而立之年，我才知道昭陵里的水，由哪儿来的，流到哪儿去。如今，步入不惑之年，我的相机里也留下了昭陵的春夏秋冬。

我渐渐懂得自己最初对昭陵的怕，不是没来由的。这里的建筑，真正体现了古代帝王建筑的哲学：非壮丽无以重威。威而生敬，当我是孩子时，并不懂得什么是敬畏，现在却深刻体会，原来最初的怕，就是一种敬畏。对这里长眠的灵魂的敬畏，对这些庄严的建筑的敬畏，对一段远去历史的敬畏。昭陵的宏伟，也正是对皇太极这位开国君主特殊地位的诠释。

我想，在这片平地上，造出一片水是好的。"水不在深，有龙则灵"，昭陵里的水，因为有了皇太极这个真龙天子，而显得更加灵秀。站在昭陵，面对这一大片碧水，不禁回想起我的人生历程。我从17岁开始过黄河跨长江，走金沙江；20岁在苏州太湖的渔船上品"太湖三白（注解1）"；28岁站在岳阳楼上回望中国第二大淡水湖洞庭湖，想起范仲淹在《岳阳楼记》中感叹"先天下之忧而忧，后天下之乐而乐"，又想起毛泽东曾为岳阳楼挥笔写下"老去有孤舟"的诗句。这

原本是杜甫的诗篇，原句是"老病有孤舟"，不过，有意也好无意也好，这一个字的差别却流露出伟人的心境。31岁时，我在西湖楼外楼上远望西湖三潭印月，吃西湖醋鱼，欣赏平湖秋月；33岁时看九寨黄龙的湖水，领略了最美的湖的风光。然而，这些大江大湖都不能在我的心上泛起涟漪。只有昭陵，那一块人工湖水，始终如镜子一样镶嵌在我的内心。

孔子曾说过，"智者乐水"（注解2），泱泱大国，正是一位智者的胸襟。昭陵，又怎么能少了水呢？从研究古建筑开始，我就更加关注昭陵里的水。我发现，这里是清皇帝陵中人工水域最大的陵寝。古代为皇帝选择"万年吉地（陵寝）"，风水很重要。风水风水，当然离不开水，既要有山，又要有水。比如关内的清西陵就有天然的大水域，雍正帝陵寝泰陵就位于五道河村，听名字就知道，那里的水有很多。正所谓"有山无水休寻地"。然而这里所说的"水"指的是"界水"两字，晋人郭璞在古本《葬经》中提到界水，正是对墓葬风水而说的，主要谈的是"地气"。"聚之使不散"说的是藏风，保持气不散；"行之便有止"说的是要形成缓流的生机，让"气"能够绵延不断地流进来，积聚在这块地上。这样一来，昭陵的一反寻常，既不依山也不傍水，而是人工造山造水，也就不奇怪了。人为弥补了风水学中的有水无山或有山无水的缺憾。水，昭陵里最重要的一部分，也是世界文化遗产的一部分，因此，保护昭陵，就必须保护好昭陵里的水。

昭陵、永陵、福陵，盛京三陵，加上已列入世界遗产名录的清东陵、清西陵，不仅构成了一组清朝帝陵体系，更是一部浓缩了清朝的历史。它们如同申遗时一样，可以说是一个不可分割的整体，研究其中任何一座陵寝，都不能孤立地去看，而必须站在整个体系基础上，只是这整体中的局部，在我心中的位置，各有千秋。走在昭陵里，头脑里幻想着皇太极智勇双全、叱咤风云的身影。一代帝王，如今安静地躺在昭陵的青山秀水间，与山相依，与水为伴，我却仿佛跨越历史的时空，在与一位智者对话。那些故事，如今都写进了历史里，也永远留在了昭陵里……

如果老的时候，还能常在昭陵的湖边散散步，我就感到满足了。

于山外堂

THE WISE TAKE PLEASURE IN RIVERS AND LAKES

I was only three years old when I toddled into Zhaoling Imperial Tomb ("Zhao" means splendor) for the first time tugging my parents' sleeves. That memory has become blurred over so long time, and I can barely recollect anything even with photos of that visit in my hands.

My later affection and obsession with Zhaoling Imperial Tomb is largely due to my mother. My five-year-old visit to Zhaoling Imperial Tomb is still vividly imprinted in the depth of my mind. At that time, students of Shenyang would go to the memorial cemetery every spring and pay respects to martyrs died in Korean War, and then a spring outing to Bei Mausoleum ("Bei" means north) would follow. I went along with my mother and her colleagues. One of my mother's colleagues showed my around on the horse tracks in Square City. I was indeed fretted when I stood on the high wall of Square City with no sight of my mother, and started begging her to take me to meet my mother. I set to sausages and bread as soon as I had my mom with me, and therefore was laughed by my mother's colleague, who regarded my begging as a clamor for food. But actually I was really scared at that time because I was not well acquainted with my mother's colleague when standing on those high walls with no sign of my mother, dark woods around and a crowd of kids in white. The dread intensified, and became impossible to constrain. I took that experience to my heart for being misunderstood, and ever since, Zhaoling Imperial Tomb was firmly fixed in my heart.

The lake water of Zhaoling Imperial Tomb stretched before my childhood eyes into infinite boundlessness. What's more, rumors of people drowning in it were often heard, and therefore people were often dreadful about the Mausoleum. I didn't walk around any of its lakes until I was a teenager, and I toured all of them by bike in my 20s. Riding by those lakes, especially in hot weather of summer, is indeed refreshing and soothing, with cold breeze stroking your back, because temperature there is lower than that inside the City. Zhaoling Imperial Tomb together with its lakes pulsates as lungs of Shenyang, bringing fresh and cool air all the time. In my 30s, I got to find sources of Zhaoling Imperial Tomb lakes and ambling directions of the water. And now when I stepped into my 40s, I have taken with my camera varied pictures of Zhaoling Imperial Tomb and treasured its scenery in my mind.

I also gradually realize that my fear of Zhaoling Imperial Tomb can be well justified. Buildings here shed illuminating lights on the architectural philosophy of ancient Chinese emperors: Magnificence and grandeur radiates stateliness. Stateliness in return evokes respect and reverence. As a child, I knew nothing as stateliness or reverence. But it occurs to me that my original fear toward Zhaoling Imperial Tomb was indeed a feeling of reverence. The reverence is a duly respect to the sleeping ancestors, sublime architectures here and their elapsing history. The magnificence of Zhaoling Imperial Tomb may also indicate the uniqueness of Hong Taiji as founding father of Qing Dynasty.

Digging a lake with tranquil and sparkling waters in Zhaoling Imperial Tomb is a brilliant idea. A Chinese saying goes like this, "The water is divine not for its depth, but for the dragon hiding in it," and waters of Zhaoling Imperial Tomb is therefore delicately beautiful for Hong Taiji. Its blue lake water reminds me of my life experience when I stand gazing it. I traversed across River Huang, Yangtze River and River Jinsha, and savored their beauty at my age of 17. I had the chance to taste "Taihu Lake Three White" (Note 1) on the fisher in Lake Tai of Suzhou when I was 20. And I also mounted Yueyang Tower and enjoyed the sight of Lake Poyang, the biggest freshwater lake in China at the age of 28, recollecting the famous lines in Odes to Yueyang Yower written by Fan Zhongyan (an outstanding scholar in North Song Dynasty), "One should be the first to worry for the future of his State and the last to claim his share of happiness," and the verse by Mao Zedong, "I am old and dying with my lonely boat." Mao's verse is

either an intentional or unknowing change of the original one by Du Fu (a poet of Tang Dynasty), "I am old and sick with my lonely boat." And the change of one word reveals the frame of Mao's mind. Later at 31, I stepped on Lou Wai Lou (restaurant name) beside West Lake in Hangzhou, overlooking Three Pools Mirroring the Moon (tourist site of West Lake) and enjoying Moon over the Peaceful Lake in Autumn (ibid) and tasting West Lake Fish in Vinegar Gravy (famous dish of West Lake). And then I visited the lake of Huanglong (a tourist site shaped like a winding yellow dragon) of Jiuzhaigou (a very famous tourist site in Sichuan Province) at 33 and got to know a beautiful lakeside scenery. But all these grand rivers and scenic lakes just fleeted away with no deep impression within my heart. On the contrary, the man-made lake of Zhaoling Imperial Tomb has been embedded in the deepest corner of my heart ever since my childhood.

The Chinese sage Confucius once observed that the wise find pleasure in streams (Note 2), and a great country like China prizes herself for broad-mindedness as a wise man. Zhaoling Imperial Tomb is never void traces of water. And ever since I took to the study of ancient architecture, I put much of attention to waters of Zhaoling Imperial Tomb. I find that water here protrudes itself as the biggest artificial water area among all imperial mausoleums of Qing Dynasty. In ancient times, geomancy was vital to the sitting of an emperors' mausoleum. Waters and mountains or hills are indispensable for such an "auspicious land." For example, West Qing Mausoleum outside Shanhai Pass resides beside a large body of natural waters, and Tai Mausoleum of Emperor Yongzheng is located in Wudaohe Village (literally Five River Village), from the name we can infer that there are a lot of waters. This coincides with a saying that "an area with hills but no waters cannot be used for burying." However, "water" here refers to the "boundary water" which was mentioned in Burial Book by Guo Pu in Jin Dynasty. Boundary water in fact is the study of geomancy, mainly talking about "geomantic energy."

"To accumulate and keep it from dispersing" means to possess the energy and keep it around while "to flow to concentrate" means to form a slow flow of life so that "energy" can continuously flow in and accumulate in one place. This is indeed peculiar with Zhaoling Imperial Tomb considering the fact that there are neither hills nestling behind nor water rippling in front, so it is easy to understand why artificial hill and waters were created, which makes up the defects of a place without mountains or waters. Water, indispensable for Zhaoling Imperial Tomb, also belongs to cultural heritage of the whole world. Therefore, protection of water is essential in preserving Zhaoling Imperial Tomb as a whole.

Three Mausoleums of Shengjing, which are Zhaoling Imperial Tomb, Yong Mausoleum and Fu Mausoleum, together with East and East Qing Mausoleums, which have been listed in the World Heritage List of UNESCO, form a system of Qing emperors' mausoleums, a condensing history of Qing Dynasty. As in the process of applying for the world cultural heritage, they are an integrity which can not be viewed separately. We must study each of them in consideration of the whole system. They are the separate parts of the whole system, but they have their own weights in my mind. While strolling around Zhaoling Imperial Tomb, the image of intelligent and resourceful Hong Taiji who fights and braves the whirlwind in history may just pop out and linger in my mind. The one-time Emperor, Hong Taiji, is lying in Zhaoling Imperial Tomb with the company of green hill and pretty lake around. And I seem to converse with him, treading through chapters of history. Those thrilling and astounding stories of Hong Taiji which go down in history still echo here.

And it would satiate my heart if I can still have chances to amble around the lakes of Zhaoling Imperial Tomb when I age into my senior years.

At Shanwai Hall

事死如生的陵寝学

和古老静谧的福陵比起来，威仪肃穆的昭陵给我的感觉更为气派庄严，它是三百多年的历史沉淀，它是悠悠古柏和红墙黄瓦隐匿的神秘。我在"一朝发祥地，两代帝王都"的沈阳出生、长大，进入昭陵的历史是从3岁开始的。而5岁时候在昭陵方城马道上，是我人生中第一次深刻感受到什么是恐惧，现在回想起来，那种感受依旧很清晰很真实。那个时候我还猜不透人生的安排，如今当已经不惑之年的我静下来回忆自己和昭陵的过往时，我觉得偌大的一个城好像藏着无数的密语，吸引着我用一生去一个一个破解，一个一个读明白。

我从小就对中国古代建筑着迷，这些年来，也做过一些这方面的研究，陵寝建筑自然是其中很重要的一部分。自古以来，中国人就很看重死亡这件事，从无数的经书典籍中我们都可以意识到。古代一直尊崇"事死如生"的丧葬原则，就是说人们把人的死亡看得等同于生一样重要，也就随之衍生出了中国独具特色的陵寝学文化。人生活在社会中有三六九等之分，遵循森严的等级制度，于是人的死亡及丧葬随之也有了明显的等级，即便是称呼都有着严格的规定。帝王的坟墓称为"陵"，圣人的坟墓称为"林"，王公贵族的坟墓称为"冢"，一般官员或富人的坟墓称为"墓"，平民百姓的坟墓则称为"坟"。封建帝王从登基那天起最为关注的事情之一，就是修建自己的陵寝。因为古人认为，修建陵寝关系到江山社稷是否会万年永固。可以说中国的陵寝学，融合了中国古代宗教学、风水学、建筑学、雕塑艺术、装饰艺术、绘画艺术等诸多文化艺术于一体。在建设陵寝过程中，以何种哲学思想为指导，是与当时的帝王的综合修养密切相关的。古代修建帝王陵寝，是国家的重要工程，在建设过程中，很多人参与，发生了很多故事，以及在后世的祭祀与守护，与朝代兴亡也有着密切的关系。

我为什么提出陵寝学这个概念，就是因为从研究古建筑开始，就十分关注古代陵寝的建筑，尤其是帝王陵寝的建筑。帝王陵寝建筑可以说是古建学中最高的学问，因为它并不是简单地涉及诸多的艺术门类，古代帝王都知道自己不可能长生不老，秦始皇13岁登基，就开始为自己修陵。历代皇帝，都是一边让人喊万万岁，一边却早早就为自己大兴土木，建造地下宫殿，希望灵魂永生，精神不死。

这些年为了研究古建筑，每到一处，我都尽量抽出时间，考察一下附近的古建筑遗迹。我探寻的足迹就这样踏访了诸多帝王将相、先圣贤民的最终归宿。去的地方有人文初祖的黄帝陵、炎帝陵、大禹陵、少昊陵、秦始皇陵、汉武帝陵、光武帝陵、唐太宗陵、唐高宗和武则天陵、宋太祖赵匡胤陵、宋神宗赵顼陵、宋哲宗赵煦陵、元成吉思汗陵、明孝陵及十三陵（注解3）等；圣人墓，著名的山东曲阜的孔林，河南洛阳老城武圣关羽的关林和湖北当阳关林；先贤名人墓，有屈原墓、岳飞墓、海瑞墓、李白墓、杜甫墓，还有喀什的香妃墓，这是我去过最西边的陵寝了。近代，更有人尽皆知的中山陵。国外，像日本的奈良、京都的天皇陵寝、青山墓园、多摩墓园等。

由于国家不同，文化也不同，西方国家的墓大都是公墓，像法国的先贤祠，是一个有强烈的宗教色彩的集体公墓。中国的丧葬文化悠久绵长，有一套完整的体制和规格，可以说是世界重要的历史文化遗产组成部分，唯一可以与之媲美的，可能只有埃及的金字塔。中国的陵寝注重风水以及福荫子孙后代。从春秋时代，孔子大力提倡"孝道"开始，厚葬之风日盛，历代不衰，并逐渐形成一套隆重复杂的祭祀礼仪和墓葬制度。上至皇帝，下至百姓，对坟墓的安置均格外重视。而为人择地卜葬的堪舆家（风水师），更以阴宅为主。唐十八座皇陵中，绝大多数都利用天然山丘，建在山岭顶峰处，居高临下，形成"南面为立，北面为朝"的形势。宋代帝陵则"头枕黄河，足蹬嵩岳"，乃"山高水来"的吉祥之地。宋陵在地形选择上与以往朝代不同，各陵皆东南高西北低。这是因为宋代盛行与汉代图宅术有关的"五音姓利"风水术，即把姓氏按五行分归五音，再按音选定吉利方位。赵，属于"角"音，利于壬丙方位，必须"东南地穹，西北地垂"。而明清以后则"宝城宝顶"，特别重视山川形胜，风水格外讲究，加之建筑的配合，皇陵的选择与规划都达到了空前的艺术水准。清朝陵寝基本是沿袭明十三陵建造的，只是相比之下关内的清东陵与清西陵与明代陵寝风格上更相近，而清东陵这块风水宝地，曾被明朝皇帝派人选看过，只是后来改朝换代，才成为清帝陵了。关外三陵虽然也有明陵遗风，但却更具满族特色。至清代，中国的陵寝学，可以说是发展至巅峰。

STUDY OF MAUSOLEUM: HONORING THE DEAD AS THE LIVING

Compared with ancient and tranquil Fu Mausoleum, Zhaoling Imperial Tomb impresses me more with its stateliness and magnificence, its sedimentary accretion of history and mystery hidden among its crusted pine trees, red walls and yellow tiles. I was born and grew up in Shenyang, a city known as cradle of a dynasty, in which two generations of emperors were born. And Zhaoling Imperial Tomb entered into my life as early as when I was three years old. And I deeply perceived the feeling of fear and awe at five when I visited Square City, standing on its horse tracks. And that perception is still fresh and vivid inside whenever I search my mind. At that time I couldn't fully comprehend that it was my karma with Zhaoling Imperial Tomb. But now at my 40s, when I recollect my attachments with Zhaoling Imperial Tomb, I sometimes deem it my fate predestined by Heaven to explore and puzzle out all the mysteries tucked around the tomb.

I have been obsessed with ancient Chinese architecture from my young age and am working at it in recent years. Mausoleum building of course falls into this field. From ancient times, Chinese people paid great attention to death and funeral, which could be proved from accounts of numerous sources such as ancient classics, books and records. In ancient China, the funeral rule of "honoring the dead as the living" had been observed and even worshiped. Death and funeral were regarded as equally significant rites as birth of life, and thus the unique culture of Chinese mausoleum and funeral was derived. People used to live in a society with strict and clear hierarchy, which was also followed in funerals. Even appellations of funeral for different social classes were named distinctly. For example, tomb of emperor was called "ling" (陵), and that of sage "lin" (林); Tomb of nobility was named "zhong" (冢), that of common government official or rich people "mu" (墓), and that of civilians was "fen" (坟). One of the biggest concerns for some emperors immediately after their enthronements was the building of their mausoleums. In the eyes of ancient people, building of mausoleums counted for much because it might impact stability and rule of a dynasty. So the culture of mausoleum in China can be regarded as an integration of religion, fengshui (geomancy), architecture, sculpture, decorative arts, painting and many others. In the process of mausoleum construction, what philosophy would be employed was closely related to the comprehensive knowledge of an emperor. What's more, the building and construction of imperial mausoleums were highlighted as major national projects. Therefore in the process of construction, the number of people involved, the stories which had happened, and the sacrifice and mausoleum guarding of future generations are all closely related to the rise and fall of a dynasty.

The reason why the study of mausoleum culture as a science comes up in my mind is that as soon as I started the study of ancient architecture, I paid close attention to ancient tomb buildings, especially the imperial mausoleum architecture. Emperors' Mausoleums were ranked as the highest knowledge in ancient architecture, because it was not just simply related to various arts. Ancient emperors knew that they could not live forever. Qin Shihuang, First Emperor of Qin Dynasty, started the construction of his mausoleum after he crowned himself at the age of 13. The emperors on one hand enjoyed the longevity courtesy paid by their subjects, and on the other hand projected their resting place as early as possible, hoping that their souls could be immortal and their spirits enjoyed eternity.

In recent years, I would spare any possible time to observe and study ancient Chinese architectural relics available wherever I go in order to enrich and further my study of the field. Hence I have visited various kinds of tombs, graves and mausoleum, the final resting place for emperors, generals and ministers of the state, sages and wise people. Tombs or mausoleums I visited include Huangdi Mausoleum (Huangdi, also Emperor Yellow, legendary ruler of ancient China), Yandi Mausoleum (Yandi, also Emperor Yan, another legendary ruler of ancient China), Dayu Mausoleum (Dayu, legendary first monarch of Xia Dynasty, best remembered for teaching the people flood-control techniques to tame China's rivers and lakes), Shaohao Tomb (Shaohao, son of Emperor Yellow and one of the mythical Five Emperors himself), Mausoleum of Qin Shihuang (First Emperor of Qin Dynasty), Mausoleum of Emperor Wudi and Tomb of Emperor Guangwudi (of Han Dynasty), Mausoleums of Emperors Taizong, Gaozong and Wu Zetian (of Tang Dynasty), Mausoleums of Emperors Taizu (Zhao Kuangyin), Shenzong (Zhao Xu, 赵 顼) and Zhezong (Zhao Xu, 赵 煦) (of Song Dynasty), Genghis Khan's Mausoleum (of Yuan Dynasty), Xiao Mausoleum (for Hongwu Emperor, founder of Ming Dynasty) and Thirteen Tombs (of Ming Dynasty) (Note 3). Other famous tombs are Confucius Family Graveyard in Qufu of Shandong Province, Guan Yu Graveyard in Luoyang of Henan Province (Guan Yu, a general serving under the warlord Liu Bei during the late Eastern Han Dynasty era of China) and Guan Yu Woods in Dangyang of Hubei Province (as head and body of Guan Yu were buried in different places). Tombs for wise men such as Qu Yuan, Yue Fei, Hai Rui, Li Bai and Du Fu are also my visiting destinations. Abakh Hoja Tomb in Kashgar, however, is the farthest that I visited in western China. Mausoleum of Dr. Sun Yatsen, a recent and well-known tomb, is of course included. I also paid visits to some famous overseas mausoleums such as mausoleums for Japanese emperors in Nara and Kyoto, Aoyama Cemetery, Tamareien Cemetery and so on.

Despite their respective distinct cultural differences in different nations, cemeteries in Western countries are mostly public, such as Pantheon of France, which is typically an open graveyard with strong religious colors. Mausoleum culture in China has a long history and it is unique in its completeness of system and specification. And nothing but the pyramids of Egypt is on a par with in this aspect. Mausoleums in China emphasize geomancy and blessings to their offspring of the tomb owners. From Spring and Autumn Period, Confucius advocated filial piety, and lavish funeral practice spread, and gradually a complex of rites and ceremonies and burial system formed. Tomb arrangement and construction were paid great attention to by people from loyal families to ordinary households. Geomancers, who chose blessed locations for people, paid much more attention to graveyards. Of the eighteen mausoleums of Tang Dynasty, most took the advantages of mountains and hills. The mausoleums, which were built on the topsides of natural hills, develop a political ideological pattern of "facing South to reign and facing North to obey," while the mausoleums of Song Dynasties, which rest emperors' heads upon River Yellow and place their feet towards Mount Song, is considered as an auspicious place of "water from high mountain." The site selection of mausoleums of Song Dynasties are quite different from that of previous dynasties with the south-east part higher than that of the north-west. Because geomantic theory of "five notes and family name" was popular in Song dynasties, which is similar with the site selection of house and grave. The theory relates family names (classified into five elements) to five notes (of the ancient Chinese five-tone scale) and the bearing of house or grave is selected accordingly. According to this theory, the shared family name of Song Emperors is Zhao and it belongs to Jiao musical scale and the blessed place for Zhao is the east and the south. So, the principle of selecting mausoleum site "higher in the southeast and lower in the northwest" must be followed. During Ming and Qing dynasties, the mausoleums were built with "surrounded walls and domes," and elegant features of mountains and rivers are emphasized, and together with the matching architecture, the selection and planning of mausoleums reach an unprecedented level. Mausoleums of Qing Dynasty basically follow the construction of Ming Tombs only with East and East Qing Mausoleums inside Shanhai Pass sharing more similar features with mausoleums of Ming Dynasty. East Mausoleum sitting was once chosen by Ming Dynasty, but with the change of dynasties, it became the tomb site of Qing Dynasty. Three Mausoleums outside Shanhai Pass have some features of Ming mausoleums, but more Manchu characteristics. The culture of Chinese mausoleums and funerals reached to its heyday in Qing Dynasty.

哲学思想决定建筑风格

对于从小就对古建筑痴迷的我来说,幸运的是,著名的清朝早期皇陵"关外三陵"就在我的生活半径之内,成为我研究古代建筑和陵寝极为有利的条件。"关外三陵"分别指永陵、福陵和昭陵。永陵位于沈阳城外的抚顺新宾满族自治县,是大清皇帝爱新觉罗氏族的祖陵。福陵在沈阳城东,昭陵在沈阳城北,沈阳人习惯称为北陵的,便是昭陵了。它是"关外三陵"中规模最大、气势最宏伟的一座,也是至今保存最完整的清陵寝。里面埋葬的是清朝第二代开国君主清太宗皇太极以及孝端文皇后博尔济吉特氏。

提起昭陵,不能不使人想到唐朝开国君主唐太宗李世民的陵寝唐昭陵,同样是开国君主,皇太极的庙号也是太宗,陵寝也叫昭陵,不能不使人猜想二者之间的联系。有人说,清昭陵就是仿制唐昭陵建造的,甚至清昭陵里面的立马石象生也是仿制唐昭陵里的"昭陵六骏"建造的。的确不能否认,清朝帝王有着希望能够像大唐王朝一样繁荣而久治的美好愿望。仔细比较就会发现,唐昭陵的六骏是浮雕,而清昭陵里的马是圆雕。不能因为名字相同,里面都有马,就将二者联系在一起。经过我的研究,我认为,清昭陵陵寝更多地继承了明朝皇陵的建筑规制,而又张扬着满族自己的文化特点。昭陵南北狭长,东西偏窄,自南向北由前、中、后三个部分组成。由南至北依次为:前部,从下马碑到正红门,包括华表、石狮、牌坊、更衣厅、宰牲厅;陵寝中部,从正红门到方城,包括华表、石象生、碑楼和祭祀用房;后部,是方城、月牙城和宝城,这是陵寝的主体。

我到过不同的国家,其文化、历史、信仰各不相同,建筑风格迥异。那么,我们国家的建筑之所以是如今这个样子,又是怎样的哲学思想促成的呢?看到如今的建筑,反思它之所以如此这般的原因,也就渐渐形成了我的对哲学思想指导下的建筑风格的研究课题。在我看来,中国陵寝设计体现的是"圣"的哲学,先人已逝而圣留心中,供奉先祖的圣明,以传子孙后代。奉先祖为"圣",既要表达对先人的尊敬和缅思,也希望得到先祖对后世基业的庇护，更是向世人展现大国国力的方式之一，因而先祖陵寝的建筑和气势自然不会丝毫逊色于宫殿庙宇。

昭陵与福陵及其他清朝皇陵比起来，建筑思想指导下的建筑风格极为相似，但又有着独特的特色。女真族是游牧民族，按习俗坟墓多建在山上。而昭陵最大的特点就是它傍水但不依山，而是直接建在平原上。现在里面的隆业山，一座人工山，全靠清朝人人工堆砌而成。原来的水域也没有这么大，智者尚水，水量充沛寓意着智慧充裕，因而人工扩大了水域。

如果把昭陵比喻成一篇气势恢宏的乐章，那它婉转起伏、渐入佳境的前奏要比福陵长很多。按长度计算，从最南端的下马碑到正红门的距离，有从正红门到皇陵距离的四倍之长。不仅前奏更为精彩，建筑规模也更大，礼制也更加完备。

PHILOSOPHIC THINKING DETERMINES ARCHITECTURAL STYLE

It's really fortunate for me who has been obsessive with ancient architecture from an early age to live near the famous three mausoleums for the first three emperors of Qing Dynasty outside Shanhai Pass in Northeast China, which provides me with convenient and favorable conditions to study ancient architecture and mausoleums. Three Mausoleums outside Shanhai Pass consist of Yong Mausoleum, Fu Mausoleum and Zhaoling Imperial Tomb. Yong Mausoleum is situated in Xinbin Manchu Autonomous County (one of the three counties under administration of Fushun City, not far from Shenyang) and it is the ancestral grave of Aisin Gioro Clan (the ruling clan of Qing Dynasty). Yong Mausoleum is located east of Shenyang City and therefore is called Dong Mausoleum ("Dong" means east). It is the mausoleum of Nurhaci (First Emperor of Qing Dynasty) and his Empress Xiaocigao. And Zhaoling Imperial Tomb is habitually called Beiling by locals because it is located north of Shenyang. Of the three mausoleums, Zhaoling Imperial Tomb is the largest in scale with imposing manner and it's also the most perfectly preserved in all royal mausoleums of Qing Dynasty. Buried inside are Hong Taiji, the second emperor of Qing Dynasty, and his Empress Xiaoduanwen, Borjigit Hala.

The mention of Zhaoling Imperial Tomb (of Qing Dynasty) may remind people of the mausoleum for Tang Taizong, founding emperor of Tang Dynasty. His mausoleum is also called Zhaoling Imperial Tomb and his posthumous title is the same as that of Hong Taiji, Taizong. Some people argue that Zhaoling Imperial Tomb of Qing Dynasty is nothing but an imitation of Tang Zhaoling Imperial Tomb and even the stone animal statues are just miniatures of those in Zhaoling Imperial Tomb of Tang Dynasty. It is undeniable that emperors of Qing Dynasty cherished the same wish of national prosperity and long period of stability. But if under careful study, distinctions of these mausoleums may be clearly identified. For example, "Six Steeds" of Tang Taizong Mausoleum are relief sculpture while stone horse of Hong Taiji Mausoleum is circular sculpture. The two mausoleums should not be associated merely for their name and the existence of stone horse sculpture. I draw a conclusion, after careful study, that Zhaoling Imperial Tomb displays unique Manchu culture while inheriting the requirements of Tang Zhaoling Imperial Tomb. Zhao Museum (of Qing Dynasty) is long from north to south while a little narrower from east to west in structure. From south to north, the Mausoleum consists of three parts: front, central and rear part. The front part consists of huabiao (ornamental pillar), stone animals, Memorial arch, dressing room and slaughter house from Dismounting Tablets to Front Red Gate. The central part consists of huabiao, stone animal statues, stele pavilion and houses for sacrificial offering from Front Red Gate to Square City. The rear part is the principal area of the Mausoleum, consists of square city, crescent city and burial bastion.

I have been to different countries, whose cultures, histories and beliefs differ from one another. Such differences are also reflected through their respective architectural style. So the study of how philosophical thoughts help shape and impact our Chinese architecture or how philosophical thoughts are reflected by architecture takes root in my mind and gradually becomes focus of my study. In my opinion, the designs of Chinese tombs embody such philosophy as worship of ancestors, whose keen intelligence and excellent judgment might remain to enlighten their offspring although they cease to exist. The worship of ancestors represents our respect and retrospect to those immortal as well as sincere wish of protection from them. It is also thought to be one definite way to exhibit national strength. Therefore, scale and magnificence of the mausoleums are undoubtedly not in the shade of those palaces and temples in Royal Court.

Compared with other emperor mausoleums of Qing Dynasty, the architectural style of Zhaoling Imperial Tomb and Fu Mausoleum is for the most part similar with that of others. But distinctions do exist. Jurchen is a nomadic tribe and it is their convention to build their tombs on hills. But the most obvious feature of Zhaoling Imperial Tomb is its building on the plain with water rippling in front but no hill nestling behind. Hill Longye (prosperity and wealth) is completely man-made by labors of that time. The original place is also dug and expanded to hold more water based on the consideration that sufficient water signifies increase of wisdom.

If compared as a symphony with tremendous momentum, Zhaoling Imperial Tomb has a much longer prelude to its climax than Fu Mausoleum. When calculated in length, the distance between Dismounting Tablet to Front Red Gate is quadrupled than that between Front Red Gate to the mausoleum vault. In addition, Zhaoling Imperial Tomb is much grander in its building scale and more integrated in its ritual system.

昭陵公园皇太极铜像／左页图
Bronze Statue of Hong Taiji inside Zhaoling Imperial Tomb Park / Left Page

少见的火葬皇陵

昭陵、福陵与清其他皇陵的重要区别之一是,努尔哈赤和皇太极死后实行的是火葬,清朝入关后除了顺治帝还沿用火葬外,其余皇帝都是土葬。

中国葬人的方法有土葬、沙葬、水葬、风葬、火葬、树葬、洞葬或天葬(注解4)等。古时绝大多数的人还是土葬,中国古代帝王死后也多是土葬。而实行火葬源于佛教的传入,但受到传统思想的深远影响,火葬只是在一些兄弟民族(注解5)地区盛行,现在辽宁抚顺的高句丽墓穴都是火葬,女真族也是其中之一。清初盛行火葬制度,因而太祖努尔哈赤、太宗皇太极及其后妃死后都是火化。实践证明,火葬,也是最科学的丧葬方式,而清朝早在三百年前就开始实行了。而入关之后,因为火葬不能被汉文化所接受,清王朝才改变了这一民族习俗。

因为是火葬,我们可以推想,在昭陵的地宫内,就不会有通常想象的帝王陵寝内巨大的棺椁,因而地宫中究竟是什么样子,就更为神秘,让人充满各种遐想了。

昭陵是清朝兴衰的缩影

昭陵是清太宗皇太极的陵寝,我对这位皇帝一直都是非常尊敬的。皇太极和他的父亲努尔哈赤比起来,更加充满智慧,是一位有魄力、有远见的杰出政治家和军事家。生活在有尚武精神的女真族中,他自小就骁勇善战。同时,他还有着常人没有的深谋远虑、运筹帷幄的管理才能,最终造就了历史上又一位昭明君主。他不仅创建了一个新的民族满族,还完善了后金的政治制度,为大清皇朝定鼎燕京,统一华夏,奠定了坚实的基础。

和众多帝王不同的是,皇太极生前一直忌讳谈论建造陵寝一事,所以这件事就一直被搁置着。1643年入关前夕,皇太极突然病故,大臣们才开始议论谋划,最终由杜如预、杨宏量等大臣(注解6)推荐,选定于盛京北部动工修建皇太极的陵寝——昭陵,基本建成用了八年的时间,面积达16万平方米。与关外三陵相比,福陵面积达19.84万平方米,永陵相对比较小,才1.1万平方米。入关之后清朝虽定都北京,但是随后的几位皇帝,尤其是康乾时期的三位皇帝,都拨大量款项,用于昭陵的改建和增修,现在的昭陵,就是经历了二百余年不断修葺形成的规模,繁盛时则大修,衰败时则简修或不修。从这一点上来看,如今的昭陵可以说是清朝后世子孙建立大清基业的发展缩影,浓缩着清朝从开始到鼎盛时期,直至最后衰亡的历史。

建筑就是凝固的历史,它将时间停滞在了曾经的某一刻,而那些斑驳的墙体,褪去的颜色,精致的雕刻,却穿越了时空,来到现在,每一次品读都是一番新的领悟。讲我对昭陵的了解,我觉得《孟子》中的那句话再适合不过。"贤者以其昭昭,使人昭昭;今以其昏昏,使人昭昭。"(注解7)身为学者的我即便穷尽一生,也不过只是"沧海一粟"的知晓。

UNUSUAL MAUSOLEUM WITH CREMATED EMPEROR

One of the important distinctions of Zhaoling Imperial Tomb and Fu Mausoleum with other Qing imperial mausoleums lies in that Nurhaci and Hong Taiji were cremated while other Qing emperors were inhumed after Manchu conquered Ming Dynasty except Emperor Shunzhi.

Ways of burying the dead abound in China, such as inhumation, sand burial, water burial, tree burial, cremation, cave burial, celestial burial (Note 4) and so on. But most people in ancient China preferred to be buried and it was also the case for most emperors. The cremation was originally introduced to China along with Buddhism. But under the impact of traditional ideas, cremation was not widely accepted apart from in some regions of minorities groups (Note 5) such as Koguryo Mural Tomb and tombs of Jurchen. Cremation was popular at early Qing Dynasty, and therefore Nurhaci and Hong Taiji and their concubines were cremated. Cremation, as the most scientific way of burial proved by later practice, was however already implemented as early as three hundreds ago in Qing Dynasty. But the practice of cremation couldn't be accepted by the majority of Han nationality and the dominant culture of the time, Qing Dynasty rules had to make a switch to burial in earth.

We can infer, considering that the owner of Zhaoling Imperial Tomb was cremated, that the underground palace of Zhaoling Imperial Tomb is not the same as the usual emperor mausoleum with huge coffin. And the mystery itself invites more vivid imagination.

ZHAOLING IMPERIAL TOMB AS A MINIATURE OF THE RISE AND FALL OF QING DYNASTY

Zhaoling Imperial Tomb is the resting place of Hong Taiji (Emperor Taizong) of Qing Dynasty, whom I have been admiring greatly. Compared with his father Nurhaci, Hong Taiji is more intelligent as daring and insightful statesman and outstanding militarist. Born and grew up in the martial Jurchen tribe, he was brave and battle-wise at an early age. And meanwhile he boasted himself with his foresighted and strategic management skills, and the perfect combination of these talents made him a shining emperor with august wisdom. His achievements in establishing a new Manchu kingdom and perfecting the political system of Later Jin Dynasty laid a solid foundation for making Yanjing (previous name for Beijing) as capital and unifying China as a whole.

Contrary to most emperors in Chinese history, Hong Taiji abstained from the topic of building his mausoleum in his lifetime, and therefore the tomb building was laid aside. However, in the year 1643, right before Jurchen conquered Shanhai Pass, Hong Taiji died of illness suddenly. The building of his mausoleum was then brought forward, and the ultimate location was selected north of Mukden (previous name of Shenyang) under the recommendation of Du Ruyu and Yang Hongliang (Note 6). Zhaoling Imperial Tomb was being under construction for 8 years, with an area of 16,000 m² while Fu Mausoleum covers an area of up to 198,400 m² and

Yong Mausoleum 11,000 m². Qing Dynasty later chose Beijing as capital, but Zhaoling Imperial Tomb was never overlooked by the subsequent emperors, especially during the reign of Emperor Kangxi and Emperor Qianlong, who appropriated large sums of money for the mausoleum's rebuilding and maintenance. The present Zhaoling Imperial Tomb is actually developed by continued expansion and renovation over a period of more than two hundred years, from which it is safe to conclude that Zhaoling Imperial Tomb stands out as the miniature of Qing Dynasty, reflecting its intact history from its incubation and rise to its collapse.

Architecture is more or less like cemented history, which captures and shuts up a particular moment in itself. Those mottled walls, washed-out colors and delicate carvings have penetrated through time, leaving behind signs of history. My understanding of Zhaoling Imperial Tomb can be summed as a line from Mencius, "A man of virtue would make clear first by himself, and then teach others. Nowadays, some people are not clear even themselves, but they want to make others understand." (Note 7) I hope to shed some lights on your understanding of the mysteries of Zhaoling Imperial Tomb with my limited findings.

昭陵公园皇太极铜像
Bronze Statue of Hong Taiji inside Zhaoling Imperial Tomb Park

"官员人等至此下马" 碑／左图
"Officials of any Rank and Common People Dismount Here" Tablet / Left

皇帝至此下马

昭陵一共有六座下马碑，立在沈阳军区门前附近的两座下马碑，上面用满、蒙、汉、藏、维五种文字刻着："诸王以下官员至此下马"。严格意义上讲，昭陵是从这两个下马碑就开始的。至此，王爷以下的官员，都必须下马，而王爷和皇室人员，包括皇帝，再往里走，到神桥前或正红门和东西红门附近的下马碑就必须下马了，否则就是大不敬。

东西红门附近和神桥前附近的下马碑，都在陵内，而陵内这四座下马碑形制基本相同，上面都用满、蒙、汉三种文字刻着："官员人等至此下马"。我一直在想，官员人等下马，那究竟包不包括皇帝呢？按官职说，皇帝是无品级的，百官都是皇帝封的，但从历史的角度看，皇帝可以说是古代最高级别的官了。皇帝如果在此不下马，那他在哪里下呢？按理说，皇帝也是该在此下马的，坐轿进祖宗陵寝，怎么也不够尊敬。中国的皇帝一向是以孝治天下的，是天下忠孝的楷模，除非年迈或者身体不适，否则进祖宗陵寝，他肯定是要比一般人更注重礼仪。也有说，皇帝不走正红门，从东红门进，那君门，这种象征级别的建筑岂不成了空设？不仅正红门成虚设，其他如御厕、更衣厅等都成了虚设。

我从事品牌学研究，每两年主持举办一次《中国品牌年鉴》编审会。每次我都会带参加编委会的评委来到昭陵参观。每次来到这儿，昭陵公园都是免票的，还专门开了通勤口让专家的车辆经过下马碑，开到华表前。清朝时过了这个下马碑，即便是帝王也是要下马步行的，而如今我们的车已经被允许开过了皇帝的下马碑。此等礼遇，在清朝时期是无法想象的。

在昭陵摄影，是我生活中的一种消遣，已经二十余年了。后来，昭陵申请世界文化遗产和申报人居环境奖，我想我的这些照片可能用得上，就义务给昭陵公园使用了。这样，和昭陵公园的工作人员就熟悉起来，待我也很热情，每次我带专家来，他们都会特别重视。但我想，之所以有这些特殊的礼遇，是出自对所有前去参观的专家，是对《中国品牌年鉴》全体和知识本身的尊重。

提到下马碑，我们大多并不陌生，在北京的很多地方，至今还可以看到这样的下马碑。在古时，很多达官贵人府上，旧时宫殿和孔庙前，甚至是一些大户人家门前，上马石、下马碑再平常不过。在当时，它是一种显示封建等级礼仪的标志。上面的碑文虽然不尽相同，但是意思是一样的，就如同现在"禁止通行"的黄色警示牌。在我研究中国广告史时，我曾专门讲过碑刻。在我看来，石碑上面的碑文是古代中国一种户外广告的形式，上面的碑文起着提示来人的作用。什么时候立起第一座石碑，现在已经很难考证了，但这种石刻"广告"在两千多年前的秦国历史上就有了相关记载。泰山上立着的无字碑，一种说法是当年秦始皇所立，不论这种说法是否成立，但是我们由此可以推断，在秦国时就已经有立碑的历史了。

昭陵的这六块下马碑则立在平原上，福陵也有四座下马碑，立在山上，离东红门和西红门很近；永陵只有两座。

DISMOUNTING TABLET — THE SPOT WHERE EVEN EMPERORS NEED TO DISMOUNT

There are altogether 6 dismounting tablets for Zhaoling Imperial Tomb, two of which are erected in front of Shenyang Military Area now. The tablets are engraved in Manchu, Mongolian and Chinese "Officials ranked lower than royal highness dismount here." Strictly speaking, the boundary of Zhaoling Imperial Tomb in Qing Dynasty started right from these two dismounting tablets. Officials with lower ranks than royal highness should dismount and walk to show their respects while Emperor and other royal members are allowed to ride further inside. But they should dismount in front of the dismounting tablets of Spirit Bridge, Front Red Gate, East and West Red Gates. Otherwise, they would be considered profane to their ancestors.

The dismounting tablets near East and West Red Gates and Spirit Bridge are located inside Zhaoling Imperial Tomb, on which are inscribed with Manchu, Mongolian and Chinese in similar format "Officials of any rank dismount here." I have been wondering whether emperors are included in "officials of any rank." Emperors as highest rulers should designate other officials but bore no official grade themselves. Emperors were not meant to dismount literally here, then where would the dismounting place be? But under Chinese ethics, emperors should dismount here to show their respect and esteem to ancestors. And emperors of China often alleged that they ruled the country under the principle of filial respect to parents and they boasted themselves examples of piety. They would then pay more attention to ceremonial sacrifices unless they were too old or sick. Some people may think that Emperor Door of Front Red Gate, symbol of hierarchy, are actually nominal, for emperors usually went in through East Red Gate. These kind of nominal buildings do exist, such as Imperial Toilet and Dressing Room.

I have worked on brandology, and every two years an editorial meeting for China Brand Yearbook is held in Shenyang. Whenever I lead the judging panel here to visit Zhaoling Imperial Tomb, we can enjoy the privilege of free tickets as well as riding past the dismounting tablet to Huabiao without alighting the vehicle. Even emperors should dismount at the dismounting tablet in Qing Dynasty, but nowadays we can pass without getting off! It is really a courteous reception unimaginable in old times.

I have been taking photos in Zhaoling Imperial Tomb for over twenty years, which is my way of recreation. Afterwards, when Zhaoling Imperial Tomb applied for the World Cultural Heritage and Habitat Environmental Award, I contributed my photos for the application. Therefore, I get acquainted with the working staff of Zhaoling Imperial Tomb Park and they of course attach special importance to the visits under my guidance. But I realize later that their hospitality is not directed to me, but to the expert panel and China Brand Yearbook.

Most of us might not feel strange to dismounting tablets, which are frequently seen in many places of present-day Beijing. And in ancient times, dismounting tablets and mounting stones were commonplace. They could be found in front of mansions of prominent officials and eminent personages, palaces and temples, and even houses of some rich people. At that time, dismounting tablets were regarded as mark of feudal etiquette and hierarchy. Their epigraphs inscribed might be different, but their meanings and functions are similar to yellow warning signs of "no thoroughfare." I expressed my understanding of stone inscriptions when I studied history of Chinese advertising. And as for me, epigraphs of stone tablets could be deemed as a kind of outdoor advertisement of ancient China, and they could remind possible visitors to pay attention or even give them warning. It is almost impossible to trace and ascertain the exact time of the first stone tablet erected. But relevant recording has proved that the stone "advertisement" can be dated back to as early as Qin Dynasty of more than two thousand years ago. The stone tablet without inscription on Mount Tai is said to have been erected by First Emperor of Qin. The theory might seem to lack proofs, but what we can safely conclude is that history of stone tablets can be dated back to Qin Dynasty.

Six dismounting tablets of Zhaoling Imperial Tomb are erected on the flat plain and four of Zhaoling Imperial Tomb are located at the hillsides, near to East Red Gate and West Red Gate while Yong Mausoleum also has two inside. The dismount tablets in Zhao ling Imperial Tomb are unique in that those in front of Spirit Bridge have Huabiao to the north as setoff.

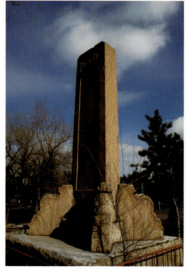 

"诸王以下官员人等至此下马"碑／左图
"Officials under Rank of Royal Highness and Common People Dismount Here" Tablet / Left
红门北侧西华表／右页图
West-side Huabiao to the North of Red Gate / Right Page

来自华表的灵感

我对昭陵的着迷,不仅是感受到整体建筑的威仪气派,也在于诸多建筑细节的精雕细琢。说来,昭陵最吸引我的,就是那六座华表了。一对立在皇帝至此下马的下马碑后面,一对立在石象生前面,一对立在石象生后面。

昭陵华表挺拔的柱身上,雕刻着精美的龙云图案,柱顶上部横插着一块云形的长片石,远远地看上去,好像柱身直插云间,给人一种庄严的感觉。华表顶端,有的有望天吼,有的只是云纹,这里的华表和天安门前的极为相似,可即使天安门前后也才有四座。和关外三陵相比,永陵内没有华表,虽然福陵也有六座华表,但是福陵的华表是清朝初期建的,选材用的是黑色石头,比较粗糙,造型也不是很优美;而昭陵的六座华表却是乾隆皇帝重修时从河北运来的石材,造型优美了很多。而关内清陵的华表,比昭陵的还要精美,可以说美轮美奂,无论是材质还是技法,都比关外要强出很多。

我设计《中国品牌年鉴》标志的灵感就来自这儿的华表,每次参加完《中国品牌年鉴》编审会的会议,我都带着评委们来到这对华表前合影。之后,带着大家参观,乐此不疲地做起了讲解员。每当我看见这些华表,一种民族自豪感就会油然而生。

碑楼北侧西华表／左页图
West-side Huabiao to the North of Stele Pavilion / Left Page
《中国品牌年鉴》编审会评委在华表前合影／上图
Photo of Judging Panel of China Brand Yearbook in Front of Huabiao / Upper

INSPIRING HUABIAO

My obsession to Zhaoling Imperial Tomb was not only due to its overall impressiveness and significance, but also its exquisite craftsmanship in details, among which six Huabiaos stand out as the most attractive to me. Two Huabiaos are erected behind the dismounting tablets of emperor, two in front of the stone animal statues and the rest two right behind the statues.

Huabiaos of Zhaoling Imperial Tomb are engraved with fine patterns of dragon clouds on their tall and straight columns, and on top of columns crosses a horizontal cloud-like stone board, which looks like a grand column soaring through clouds and incurs majesty when looked from afar. On top of some Huabiaos sits a mythical creature called hou (also called "denglong", one of nine sons of Dragon, which has the habit of looking up into sky. Hous on top of Huabiaos is said to be responsible for communication between people and Heaven). On top of some other Huabiaos are inscribed with patterns of cloud. Huabiaos here are rather similar to those in front of Tiananmen Square, around which there are altogether only four. There are no huabiao in Yong Mausoleum, while there are six in Fu Mausoleum and Zhaoling Imperial Tomb respectively. However the Huabiaos in Fu Mausoleum were sculpted with grey stone in early Qing Dynasty and so look coarse and less graceful, while those in Zhaoling Imperial Tomb were made of stone transported from Hebei when Zhaoling Imperial Tomb was renovated under the care of Emperor Qianlong, and they are more beautifully shaped. Huabiaos of the mausoleums inside Shanhai Pass are more exquisitely carved, which are much better not only in terms of materials but also in terms of techniques than those outside the Pass.

My inspiration in designing the logo of China Brand Yearbook comes right from Huabiaos here. Whenever we have editorial meetings of China Brand Yearbook, I will invite all members of the judging panel to take photos in front of these Huabiaos, and then show them around as a tour guide happily. Whenever I lay my eyes on them, my national pride arises spontaneously.

神桥南东华表／上图
East-side Huabiao to the South of Spirit Bridge ／ Upper
红门内东华表／右页图
East-side Huabiao inside Red Gate ／ Right Page

清西陵（慕陵）神桥 第三座／左上图
Spirit Bridge of West Qing Mausoleum (Mu Mausoleum), Number Three / Upper Left

神桥南面西侧石狮／右上图
Stone Lion Statue at the West Side of Spirit Path to the South of Spirit Bridge / Upper Right

昭陵神桥／右图
Spirit Bridge of Zhaoling Imperial Tomb / Right

连接阴阳两界的神桥

经过前面的华表，是一对石狮，再往北面是一座神桥。一般，陵前的桥多修为拱桥，但昭陵内该有曲线弧度的"拱桥"前面却是平的。

昭陵的神桥，桥身宽大，一桥三洞，青砖铺面，今改为条石。以昭陵来说，陵寝地势基本是前低后高，这样，每到雨季必然有大量的雨水从后向前泄出，神桥的玉带河变成了排水的渠道，起到保护陵寝的作用。

神桥下那片极宽阔的水域，面积东大西小，呈葫芦形，神桥就正好嵌在河面最窄的掐腰处。这样的情况在很多皇家陵寝前都可以见到，也不知道是不是人们有意而为之，我想应该包含着更深刻而我们后人还没参透的学问吧。昭陵内的这座神桥与福陵神桥最大的不同是，昭陵神桥在红门外，福陵神桥在红门内，福陵神桥是旱桥，桥下面并没有流水流过，只起到象征性作用。我一直以为关外三陵中，永陵是没有神桥的，后来发现永陵也有神桥，在第一道栅栏门那，有一个一尺多宽的沟，桥几乎不易被人发现。陵寝内的桥，一般都是礼制建筑，并不是为了交通实用而建，而是希望搭建连接阴阳两界的精神桥梁。

在昭陵内建造这座神桥，表面看来是起着连接作用的，其实其中深意不仅如此，还包含着建桥者的"别有用心"。明清皇陵建桥造梁的历史由来已久，这主要是受到当时风水学和建筑哲学思想的影响。修为拱桥，这样人走路的时候就要弯曲膝盖，弓下腰，卑躬屈膝地向前走，自然而然成了叩首的样子。河北清代陵内的拱桥一般都是平的，比如慕陵，这是因为道光帝觉得愧对天下百姓，无颜再受后人拜谒。不过关内的清陵中一般都有金水桥，甚至类似正红门那样等级森严的神桥、君桥、臣桥；而关外三陵中，则没有那么多桥，这可能与地形也有一定关系。关内清陵一般都有较大的天然水域，而关外三陵则没有，一般都是人工水域。关内清代陵寝主要分为清东陵与清西陵，道光帝的慕陵位于清西陵，最初陵寝地址选在东陵，后因发现地宫浸水，便改在西陵重建。而我们现在看到的昭陵也不是昭陵全貌，因为在河北还有一座昭西陵，按体制，昭西陵应属于沈阳昭陵。关于昭西陵，历史留给我们很多疑问。而沈阳昭陵内的桥又为什么是平的呢？我现在还尚不得知，可越是不知便越想知，还是留给我以后继续研究吧。

神桥
Spirit Bridge

SPIRIT BRIDGE, LINK BETWEEN LIFE AND DEATH

Passing Huabiaos, visitors may come across a pair of stone lions, and further north is Spirit Bridge. There are usually built arch bridges in front of imperial mausoleums, but here the front part of the so-called arch bridge has no circular line and becomes flat.

Spirit Bridge of Zhaoling Imperial Tomb is wide in body with three archways. The bridge road used to be covered with black bricks, but it is now changed to block stone. The terrain of Zhaoling Imperial Tomb is low in the front and high at the back, and therefore, in rainy season a great deal of rainwater floods to the front. The Jade Belt River under Spirit Bridge plays the role of drainage, thus protecting the Mausoleum from being flooded. Inside the Mausoleum, there are some artificial or natural ditches, upon which Spirit Bridges are built for drainage.

The wide expanse of water under Spirit Bridge shapes like a gourd with the east part larger in area than the west part, and the Bridge is built right at the narrowest place of the river like the waist of gourd. The structure is frequently found in many imperial mausoleums, and it is still an enigma whether it is arranged on purpose or just a coincidence. There might be deeper connotation needing our further exploration. The biggest difference lies in the fact that Spirit Bridge of Zhaoling Imperial Tomb is built outside Red Gate while that of Fu Mausoleum is a dry bridge with no flowing water underneath inside Red Gate, which is merely a symbol. I had thought that there was no spirit bridge inside Yong Mausoleum. But later I found the inconspicuous bridge near the first barrier gate on a narrow ditch over one chi (Chinese traditional unit of length, equal to 1/3 meter). Bridges inside imperial mausoleums are built out of etiquettes rather than actual traffic purpose. They are deemed as a link between life and death.

Spirit Bridge of Zhaoling Imperial Tomb is more than a link of two separated parts of the mausoleum. Bridge builders also had ulterior motives. It was a common practice to build bridges inside imperial mausoleums in Ming and Qing Dynasties, which was influenced by fenshui and architectural philosophy of that period. Ascending an arch bridge requires people to bend over and kneel down as if to bow and kowtow to show their respect. The arch bridges of Qing Dynasty inside Hebei Province are generally flat, because Emperor Daoguang of Qing Dynasty felt that he did not deserve respect from his civilians. Generally speaking, there are Golden Water Bridges in mausoleums of Qing Dynasty, and there are even spirit bridges, emperor bridges and official bridges, which are the symbols of hierarchy like the gates inside Front Red Gate. But there aren't so many bridges in Three Mausoleums outside Shanhai Pass, which may result from different terrains, because there are larger natural waters under bridges inside Shanhai Pass, but only artificial waters outside the Pass. Mausoleums of Qing Dynasty inside Shanhai Pass are mainly divided into East Mausoleums and West Mausoleums. Mu Mausoleum of Emperor Daoguang sits inside West Mausoleums, which was initially planned to build in the East Mausoleums, and later reconstructed in the West because of water soaking in the underground palace there. What we see now about Zhaoling Imperial Tomb is not its panorama, because there is also a West Zhaoling Imperial Tomb in Hebei Province. According to the system, West Zhaoling Imperial Tomb belongs to Zhaoling Imperial Tomb in Shenyang. History left us a lot of puzzles about West Zhaoling Imperial Tomb. But the reason why the bridge in Zhaoling Imperial Tomb was flat is still unknown. I can't figure it out either, which arouses my curiosity deeply for later study.

无名牌坊

昭陵前部是从下马碑到正红门,包括华表、石狮、石牌坊、更衣厅、宰牲厅等建筑群。

正红门前立着的,是昭陵内唯一的石牌坊。昭陵牌坊数量比福陵少一个,福陵两个石牌坊是东西向的,又叫下马石牌坊,和下马碑有着同样功能,形制上更像是沈阳故宫前的两个木牌坊;而昭陵石牌坊是南北向的。但昭陵中的这个牌坊比起福陵来,材料更好,雕刻之精细也堪称一绝。关外三陵中,永陵没有牌坊。关外清陵中的牌坊比起关内清陵中的牌坊略有不同。清陵中,牌坊最多的应属关内雍正帝陵寝泰陵,三座牌坊并立。关外昭陵内的牌坊,是一座仿木架结构的四柱三间三楼牌坊,远远看过去,气势磅礴,令人震撼。令我百思不解的是,一般古代牌坊都是有字的,或是人名,或是记载功德等,而昭陵坊额上却没有任何文字。我从十几岁就开始寻找上面的字,但至今也没发现任何字迹。这成了我心中的未解之谜。无名牌坊经过两百余年的岁月,据说有点倾斜,有人为了保护这座古迹,特意前后用了六根铁杆子将其支撑着,整座牌坊看起来像拄着拐杖,我觉得这种做法并不科学,有点画蛇添足的味道。

牌坊有着悠久的历史,《诗经》中就有关于牌坊的记载,只是那时叫衡门。在唐朝的时候,朝廷不允许沿街两侧有商店,就选定一条街为商业街,规定小商贩在指定的街内卖东西,通常那时在这样的街两端,各立一个牌坊,以示标志。东市、西市就是唐朝兴盛繁荣一时的著名商业街,我们常说的"买东西",有人推测就是源自这儿的。如今,在很多城市繁华的商业街,我们还能看到这种形式的牌

无名石牌坊／上图 Anonymous Stone Memorial arch／Upper
无名石牌坊旧照（赵琛 藏）／下图 Old Picture of Anonymous Stone Memorial arch(Collected by Zhao Chen)／Lower

坊，例如南京的夫子庙。

在我著述的广告史中，也提到过牌坊。牌坊，民间也叫作牌楼（注解8）。但这里的"楼"和我们理解的居住的楼不同，它虽名为楼，属于建筑，但是却没有使用价值，一不能乘凉，二不能居住，只是起到组织空间、点缀景观的作用。在我看来，牌坊是古代社会最高级别的广告形式。因为建牌坊须由朝廷批准或皇帝御赐，是不能擅自建筑的，而多用于宣扬封建礼教、标榜功德等。不论是整体造型设计，还是雕刻技法，都极其考究，山东单县的百狮坊、百寿坊就是很好的例子。在古代民间，形式各异的牌坊是普遍存在的。众所周知的北京东单、西单、东四、西四，几处热闹的商业区，都是因为有过一座或四座牌坊而得名的。

昭陵里面很多建筑对我的吸引力，在我很小的

无名石牌坊 / 左图
Anonymous Stone Memorial arch / Left
无名石牌坊前石狮 / 上图
Stone Lion in Front of Anonymous Stone Memorial arch / Upper

时候就有。少年的时候,我常常一个人,坐半天时间的公交车,绕了半个沈阳城,来昭陵写生。有一幅积雪下的牌坊就是那个时候画的。那幅画还在当时的沈阳少年宫展出过,插曲是,我记得明明是我的作品,却写上了别人的名字,我特意找老师去说明情况,可是老师并不太在意我一个小孩的话,后来还是我父亲去了才改过来。最终证书发下来名字还是错的。人越长越大,读的书也多了起来,事情更是经历了不少,才知道历史上张冠李戴的事情实在是太多了,历史上忠奸颠倒的事情更是现在人无法知晓和辨识的了。小孩子的时候较真,就非要弄个子寅卯丑来不可,而今站在历史长河中再看看,我这点儿小事又算得了什么呢?错了名头的事情在我这些年的生活中也不少见。还是郑板桥的那四个字发人深省啊:难得糊涂。

在牌坊和正红门的西侧,是宰牲厅,这里是祭祀时用来宰杀牲口的场所。宰牲厅里面原来有三口釜,一口铜铸的,两口铁铸的。釜,是祭祀时用来煮肉的。铜釜即铜铸的大锅,昭陵里的这口铜釜,口径1.5米,腹深0.56米,釜外有八个兽形环。现在作为文物保存在仪仗房内。宰牲厅前,原来还有一口井,现在盖了一个水泥盖子,应该把它修复了。在关内,清陵中的宰牲厅,都称为"神厨库",只是位置上与关外相反,关外宰牲厅在正门西侧,关内神厨库在正门的东侧,在功能用途上与关外的宰牲厅是一样的。

ANONYMOUS MEMORIAL ARCH

The front part of Zhaoling Imperial Tomb refers to the area from Dismounting Tablets to Front Red Gate, which consists of such buildings as Huabiao, stone lion, stone Memorial arch, dressing house and slaughter house.

Memorial arch in front of Front Red Gate is the only one inside Zhaoling Imperial Tomb, one less than Fu Mausoleum. The two stone Memorial arches of east-west direction in Fu Mausoleum are also called Dismounting Memorial arch, playing the same role as dismounting tablets, and they resemble in form the two wooden Memorial arches in front of Mukden Palace. Memorial arch in Zhaoling Imperial Tomb is of north-south direction with better material and finer engraving. Of Three Mausoleums outside Shanhai Pass, Yong Mausoleum is the only one without Memorial arch. There is slight differences between Memorial archs in Qing mausoleums outside Shanhai Pass and those inside Shanhai Pass. Among Qing Mausoleums, Tai Mausoleum of Emperor Yongzheng has the most Memorial arches, with three of them standing side by side. Memorial arch of Zhaoling Imperial Tomb outside the Pass follows the structure of wooden Memorial arch with 4 pillars, 3 bays and 3 arch rooftops, and therefore looks grand and magnificent if watched from afar. But what puzzles me is that there are no characters, names or description of merits and virtues on it, for these are usually essential in ancient Memorial arches of China. I started my searching of characters of any kind, but in vain, which becomes a riddle in my mind. The anonymous Memorial arch tilted a little after over two hundred years, and therefore is popped up with 6 steel poles. But that makes it look like a person with a crutch, unnecessary and unscientific.

Memorial arch has a long history with early recordings in The Book of Poetry with a name of "Beam Door." In Tang Dynasty, shops and stores were prohibited along streets, then the imperial court chose one particular street for commercial purpose, along which selling goods were permitted. Usually at either end of such a street, a Memorial arch would be erected as a sign. The east market and west market were once prosperous business street in Tang Dynasty, from which some scholars conjecture that the Chinese phrase "mai dong xi" (which means buying stuff) is thus originated. And nowadays, this type of Memorial arch can still be found in the bustling business streets of many cities, such as Confucius Temple in Nanjing.

In my book regarding history of advertising, I also deal with Memorial arches. Memorial arch is also called Pailou (see Note 8), but it is just used for exhibition and ornament rather than shelter or accommodation, and has no practical value. In my opinion, Memorial arch is the superlative type of advertising in ancient China. It couldn't be built unless approved by imperial court or emperor edict, and its function was to preach feudal ethical codes or eulogize merits and virtues. Memorial arch is extremely fastidious both in its overall structure and engraving details, and Baishou Fang and Baishi Fang of Shanxian County in Shandong Province are good exemplifications of their delicacy and intricacy. Memorial arch of various forms were indeed common in ancient China. For instance, such well-known commercial districts in Beijing as Dongdan, Xidan, Dongsi, Xisi were all originally named after Memorial arches.

Many buildings inside Zhaoling Imperial Tomb appeal to me, even since my childhood. I would come to Zhaoling Imperial Tomb for sketches after a long ride through half Shenyang on buses all by myself. A sketch of Memorial arch covered with heavy snow was drawn on one of those occasions, which was even put on display in Shenyang Children's Palace. But what made the sketch really impressive was the episode that it was signed a wrong name. I went to my teacher to explain the error, but was ignored for being considered childish. Later, signature of the sketch was corrected under the protest and persistence of my father. But the name on the certificate of award was unfortunately wrong again. As I grew up, I read more books, experienced and tasted ups and downs in life. And I got to know that in history confusion of one thing with another happened all the time, and even the most loyal were often twisted as treacherous. So the mistaken signature on my sketch was in fact nothing worthy of mention. Even nowadays mischievous things do exist in our daily occurrences. So the line by Zheng Banqiao (painter of Qing Dynasty), is really enlightening and thought-provoking, "where ignorance is bliss, it's folly to be wise."

On the west side of Memorial arch and Front Red Gate is slaughter house, where animals were killed for sacrifices. There used to be three fus (a kind of cauldron used in ancient China) inside with one cast out of copper and two out of steel. Fu was used to boil meat on occasion of sacrifices. The copper fu has a diameter of 1.5 meters, depth of 0.56 meter and eight animal hoops on it. It is now kept in Honor Guards House as cultural relic. There used to be a well in front of slaughter house, which is covered by a cement lid now. Renovation and repair are necessary in order to show visitors how it looked like before. Inside Shanhai Pass, slaughter houses of Qing mausoleums are all called Holy Cook Houses, whose location are opposite to those outside shanhai Pass: those inside the Pass are located in the west side of the main entrance while those outside the Pass in the east side. However, both Slaughter houses and Holy Cook Houses share the same functions and purposes.

无名石牌坊／左页图
Anonymous Stone Memorial arch / Left Page
无名石牌坊上八宝图案／下图
Patterns of Eight Treasures of Anonymous Stone Memorial arch / Lower

罕见的水冲御厕

牌坊和正红门之间有一处东所，平时不对游人开放。这里面有一个非常有趣的设施，是残留下来的御厕，它是目前保存最完好的一座古时蹲便，用一块巨石雕刻而成。这在古代陵寝中专为祭祀用的水冲厕所是极为罕见的。申遗以后，这里和福陵里的"齐班房"、"饽饽房"遗址一样都用玻璃罩保护起来，保护是对的，但是这种方法是否科学，我想还值得商榷。

很多去过北京故宫、沈阳故宫，或是众多皇陵的人，都会纳闷，怎么偌大的院子找不到一个厕所呢？按照古代的习俗礼仪，"这种污物不能安置在房间里"的，所以当时皇帝方便时一般都是用马桶的。现在沈阳故宫东所的颐和殿东侧和西所的迪光殿西侧，有两处御厕，里面放的就是马桶，马桶是需要人去倒脏物的，而不是水冲的；昭陵里的这座御厕，却是用水冲的。在陵寝中设置厕所并不是新鲜的事，在汉代就有，现在出土的汉墓中，就有两边有扶手的象征性的厕所。

提起御厕，让我想起一段小经历：我在日本游历讲学的时候，就注意到，日本公用厕所配有音乐的有趣现象。在日本尤其是在商场，日本人上厕所时一般都要排队，厕所内的空间比较小，为了避免上厕所时发出的声音被外面的人听到，场面尴尬，日本人就想出了安装厕所音乐盒的方法，盖住了上厕所时发出的不雅声音。一次，我带一些日本朋友参观昭陵，并给他们做导游。走到东所这个御厕的时候，我特意对日本朋友讲，厕所旁配乐的方式在中国早就有了。指着这个御厕，我让日本朋友猜猜皇帝如厕时奏什么曲子，大家也都面面相觑，猜不出来。我灵机一动，信口说道："据说皇帝出行，上厕所时用的是帐篷，为了避免出声响，奏乐的人给皇帝奏'高山流水'，给皇后奏'雨打芭蕉'"。听到我的玩笑话，大家都哈哈大笑起来。今天，我们为了游人方便，在方城东南角楼的东侧修了游人的公厕，我们今天的待遇比古代皇帝都高。

御厕影壁／左页图
Screen Wall of Imperial Toilet／Left Page
御厕影壁旧照／左上图
Old Picture of Screen Wall of Imperial Toilet／Upper Left
更衣房院门／右上图
Gate of Dressing House／Upper Right
御厕门旧照／左下图
Old Picture of Imperial Toilet Door／Lower Left
御厕外更衣房遗址／右下图
Relics of Dressing Room outside Imperial Toilet／Lower Right

UNUSUAL IMPERIAL TOILET WITH FLUSHING SYSTEM

Right between Memorial arch and Front Red Gate, there is a relic, which is rarely open to tourists. There is a very funny facility inside, the relic of an imperial toilet stool, which is the most intact of its kind. It is carved out of a big stone. After application of Zhao ling Imperial Tomb as World Heritage, the imperial stool of Zhaoling Imperial Tomb, together with Qi Ban Fang (Tomb Guards House), Bo Bo Fang (Pastry House) of Fu Mausoleum are protected with glass shields. Protection of these sites is of course necessary, but the method is negotiable.

Many people who have visited Forbidden City in Beijing, Mukden Palace in Shenyang, or many imperial mausoleums may wonder why no toilet can be found in these places. According to rites of ancient China, stool was deemed filthy and couldn't be fixed inside a room. Therefore, emperors usually used portable toilet. There are two imperial toilets to the east of Yihe Hall (Harmony Hall) and to the west of Diguang Hall (Edification Hall) in Mukden Palace, and portable stools are placed inside the two

御厨原有屋顶结构 /1 图
Original Roof Structure of Imperial Toilet / Picture 1
御厨旧照 /2 图
Old Picture of Imperial Toilet / Picture 2
御厨屋顶旧照 /4 图
Old Picture of Imperial Toilet Roof / Picture 4
御厨遗址 /3 图、5 图
Relic of Imperial Toilet / Picture 3, Picture 5

toilets. These toilets and stools need to be poured and cleaned manually while the toilet in Zhaoling Imperial Tomb has water flush facility. Actually, equipping toilets in mausoleums is nothing new at all, and such practice can be traced back to Han Dynasty. In some unearthed tombs of Han Dynasty, symbolic toilets with rails on both sides can be found.

I have an anecdote to share regarding the imperial toilet. When I was invited for lectures in Japan, I noticed an interesting phenomenon. Toilets of Japan are often dubbed with background music, especially in shopping malls. Japanese people usually have to line up for their turns in toilets, which are often small places. So in order to avoid embarrassment of unwanted sound, the toilets usually have music as background. So the indelicate sound can be covered up by way of playing background music. So when I once showed several Japanese friends around

宰牲厅 /1 图
Slaughter house / Picture 1
御厨外影壁旧照 /2 图、3 图
Old Pictures of Screen Wall of Imperial Toilet / Picture 2, Picture 3
宰牲厅院内水井旧照 /4 图
Old Picture of Well inside Slaughter house / Picture 4
宰牲厅院内水井 /5 图
Well inside Slaughter house / Picture 5
定东陵慈禧墓下马碑 /6 图
Dismounting Tablet of Empress Cixi Tomb in Dingdong Mausoleum / Picture 6
宰牲厅铁锅 / 右页图
Boiler of Slaughter house / Right Page

Zhaoling Imperial Tomb, I specially explained that "toilet with background music" had already appeared long time ago in China. Pointing at the imperial toilet to the east of Yihe Hall, I encouraged Japanese guests to make a guess of the melody played inside when emperors were answering the nature's call. And they were surely puzzled and completely at loss. A bright idea occurred to me on the spot, and I told them that draperies was used to shelter the emperor or empresses when they traveled outside. In order to cover unwanted sound, music players would perform "Lofty Mountains and Flowing Water" for emperors and "Raindrops Come Patteringly Ceaselessly on the Banana Leaves" for empresses. People laughed at my tricky figuration. Nowadays, a modern toilet is built in southeast turret of Square City for tourists, much better than the imperial toilet.

正红门／左图
Front Red Gate / Left
［通高8.775米，城墙高 2米］
(8.775 meters high overall with 2-meter-high wall)
正红门前神道御壁（《古建筑词典》）／上图
Imperial Wall of Spirit Path in Front of Front Red Gate (from *Dictionary of Ancient Architecture*)/Upper

正红门的学问

站在石牌坊下，面朝北，就是昭陵陵寝的总门户——正红门。正红门又称大红门，它建于顺治八年（1651年），位于整个陵园的正南位置，是陵园的正门。大红门建在须弥座式台基之上，台基前后分别有三路台基，通向陵前陵内。大红门是单檐歇山式顶，顶满铺黄色琉璃瓦，由三个半圆形的红色拱形门洞组成。门洞上方的券脸石上雕刻着二龙戏珠图，下部雕刻有寿山、福海、松树、宝瓶、荷花等吉祥图案，皇家气派咄咄袭来。门楣正中嵌有长方形的石雕门额，门额光素无字。每间门洞中间是对开的两扇红门，门上饰六角形兽面铺首，门扇两面都有金色门钉。虽然昭陵内的神桥是平的，但从牌坊上正红门有一段台基要蹬，前来拜谒皇陵的人自然在这里，还是要卑躬屈膝地前进了，也不知道是不是有意这样安排，如果是，那这建筑者可真有智慧。福陵的正红门就在广场上，没有落差，门扇上没有门钉；而永陵则没有正红门，只有一道栅栏门，也没有门钉。而正门的颜色也是有说法的，不是所有清代帝王陵寝的正门都是红色的，比如关内清陵，有的甚至没有红门与红墙，如道光帝的慕陵和慈禧的定东陵，是灰黄色墙与门，这也是清朝皇家谦虚罪己的一种方式。有的，则没有琉璃袖壁，如顺治帝的孝陵。

我见过门洞最多的是天安门，有五个门洞，象征九五至尊，而昭陵、福陵的正红门都有三个门洞，东西红门却只有一个门洞。为什么正红门有三个门洞，不是五个门洞呢？这里也大有学问，正红门三个门洞的名字分别叫君门、神门、臣门。听名字就知道,使用上有严格的等级规定。神门、君门、臣门,不同的人出入不同的门,这种做法,突出了皇权的至高无上。正中一间被称为"神门",这是皇太极与其皇后孝端文皇后神灵出入的门户,是帝后的棺椁神牌等通过的门。神门平时不开,只在昭陵举行大祭的时候才打开,但除了抬祭品及送祝版等祭祀用品的官兵可以从神门入陵,其余任何人不允许从此门进入。现在在很多电视剧中经常看到扮演皇帝的演员大摇大摆地从正中间的门进入,这是对历史文化的无知造成的错误。旁边的君门和臣门才是给皇帝及大臣们走的。我们今天走的都是当年皇帝祭祖时走的君门,这在当时是越制的,后果是不堪设想的。

ENIGMA OF FRONT RED GATE

The main entrance of Zhaoling Imperial Tomb – Front Red Gate, also called Great Red Gate, comes into sight if you are standing below the stone Memorial arch and facing north. The Gate, built in the eighth ruling year of Emperor Shunzhi (1651), is located at the due south part of Zhaoling Imperial Tomb as its main entrance. It is built on Sumeru-throne base, of which there are three flights of stairs side by side in the front and at the back. Great Red Gate has single-eave gable and hip roof covered with yellow glazed tiles. It contains three semi-circle red arched gateways. There are auspicious patterns of Two Dragons Playing with a Pearl engraved on the upper face stone of the arched gateway, and mountains of longevity, oceans of happiness, pines, blessed vase, lotus flower sculptured on its lower parts, which imposes upon us imperial majesty. In the middle of the upper lintel is embedded with a rectangular stone board with nothing on it. There are two red doors in each gateway, and their doors are decorated with hexagon animal head applique as well as golden doornails. Although Spirit Bridge inside is flat, there is a flight of stone stairs to ascend from Memorial arch to Front Red Gate. It is the road that people have to pass when entering the Mausoleum, and they have to bend and stoop here on these stairs, as if its designers had purposefully and cleverly arranged in this way. The red gate of Fu Mausoleum is located right on the square, so there is no drop in elevation, and there are doornails only on one side of its doors. In contrast, there is no front red gate but a fence in Yong Mausoleum and there is of course no doornail on it. There are also rules for the color of front red gates. Not all front red gates of Qing mausoleums are red, for example, the ones in the mausoleums inside the Pass. Some mausoleums don't even have any red gates or red walls. For example, the walls and gates in Mu Mausoleum of Emperor Daoguang and East Ding Mausoleum of Cixi are yellowish grey, which is a way for Qing imperial family to show their modesty and humbleness. In contrast, no glazed screen walls are built on either side of Front Red Gate in Xiao Mausoleum.

The building with the most gateways I have ever seen is Tiananmen (or Gate of Heavenly Peace) with five archways, which used to be interpreted as symbol of emperor. So why are there only three gateways on Front Red Gate of Zhao or Fu Mausoleum instead of five while there is only one on its East or West Gate? Great Red Gate consists of three doors such as Door of Emperor, Door of Spirit and Door of Officials, by means of which strict hierarchy can be detected. People of different social hierarchy should enter the Mausoleum through different doors, which in turn reflected supremacy of the imperial power. The door in the middle is called Door of Spirit, which is deemed as gateway for the spirits of Hong Taiji and his Empress Xiaoduanwen. The Door can also be used to transport coffins and memorial tablets of emperor and empress. Door of Spirit is usually closed with only occasional exceptions of grand sacrifices in Zhaoling Imperial Tomb, and even on these occasions nobody but soldiers and officials carrying sacrificial boards and offerings can pass through. We may notice on many teleplays that actors of emperor enter the mausoleum via the middle door, which of course was a mistake caused by historical ignorance. The side doors are for emperors and officials. The door opened for tourists now is actually Door of Emperor when they offered sacrifices to their ancestors, which would lead to disastrous result in feudal society of China.

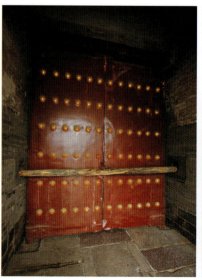 

正红门门扇南面、北面／下图
South and North of Front Red Gate / Lower

正红门门环兽头／右页图
Animal Head on Knocker of Front Red Gate / Right Page

正红门袖壁
Sleeve Wall of Front Red Gate
[袖壁长8.5米，高5米]
(8.5 meters long and 5 meters high)

来自龙壁的灵感

大红门两侧分别有一照壁，因为其建筑形式看似衣服的两个袖子，也称袖壁。袖壁为黄色琉璃瓦顶，正中嵌有一椭圆形琉璃构件，称为袖壁的盒子，壁上浮雕着姿态生动、气宇轩昂的五彩琉璃蟠龙，所以袖壁又叫龙壁或龙砖看墙。昭陵共有六对12座龙壁，如此之多的龙壁在陵寝中出现，这在明清诸陵中也是罕见的。福陵中只有4座龙壁，而永陵的4座壁是砖雕的，不是琉璃材质的，与福陵、昭陵的不同。传说龙壁有镇妖、驱邪、护陵之作用。当年我给"老边饺子"设计品牌标识的时候，灵感就来源于昭陵的龙壁。

仔细看，龙壁上刻有时间和人名，和福陵一样，都是采用实名制。我想，也正是这种实名制，才使古代建筑很少有如现代的"豆腐渣工程"。只有保证了工程质量，这些古建筑才能历经百年风雨，依然威严矗立。

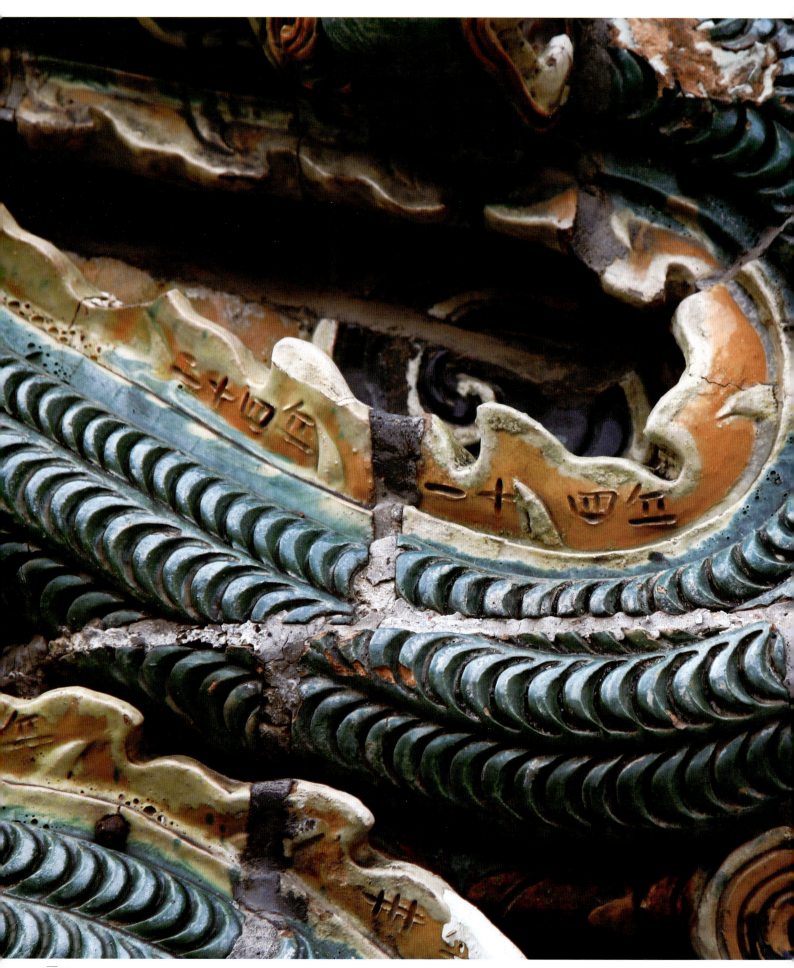

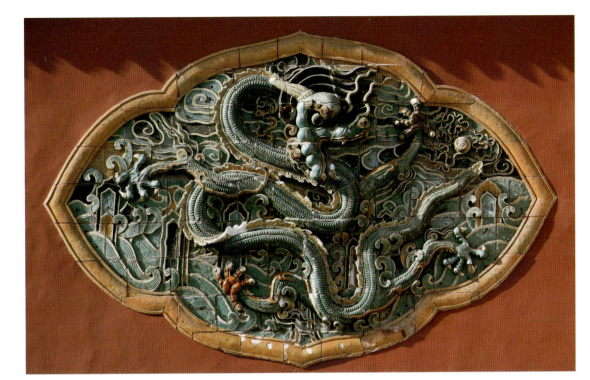

神壁蟠龙局部 ／左图
Curled-up Dragon on Sleeve Wall (Partial) / Left

正红门神壁 ／上图
Sleeve Wall of Front Red Gate / Upper

INSPIRATION FROM DRAGON WALL

There is a screen wall on either side of Great Red Gate, which is also called Sleeve Wall as it looks like a pair of sleeves of clothes in its form. Sleeve Wall has yellow glazed tiles at its top, and an elliptic glazed pattern embedded in its center, which is regarded as box of Sleeve Wall. On the wall there are relief sculptures of live and impressive curled-up dragons made out of colored glaze, and therefore they are also called Dragon Wall or Dragon Brick Screen Wall. There are altogether 12 Dragon Walls inside Zhaoling Imperial Tomb, which is really unusual in imperial mausoleums of Ming and Qing Dynasty. Fu Mausoleum has only 4 dragon walls and the 4 inside Yong Mausoleum are brick-sculptured rather than colorfully glazed in Zhaoling Imperial Tomb and Fu Mausoleum. Dragon Wall is said to be able to check demons, drive out evil spirits and protect mausoleums. My inspiration came from these dragon walls when I was asked to design brand marking of "Laobian Dumplings" (famous food brand of Shenyang).

If you look carefully at the dragon walls of these imperial mausoleums, you can find time of sculpture and real names of the sculptors. Thanks to the real-name system, quality of ancient architectures can be ensured to stand tall and upright after experiencing winds and rains for hundreds of years.

正红门神道 1
Spirit Path of Front Red Gate 1

给灵魂走的神道

进入大红门向北有三条笔直的用石板铺成的石路，正中与"神门"连接的路叫神道，它和"神门"同样是陵主"灵魂"出入陵寝走的道路。神道从正红门一直通向陵寝后部月牙城的影壁前，是全陵的中轴线。陵寝主体建筑全部建在南北中轴线上，其他附属建筑则均衡地建在它的两侧。按清陵寝制度，从大红门至隆恩门中间必须有建筑物将两者隔断，寓意"风水"一眼望不断。在古人看来，祖陵"风水"的好坏，直接影响皇位的传承和龙脉的延续，事关重大。因此明清陵寝多在神道上修设"影壁山"及"龙凤门"遮挡。昭陵神道未使用影壁山，而是在神道上建神功圣德碑碑楼，也形成"风水"一眼望不到头的效果。神道也和神门一样神圣不可侵犯，除了大祭时抬祭品、送祝版、祝帛的官兵可以行走之外，其他人禁止随意乱行，在清代有"横走罚，竖走杀，马走割蹄"的规矩。

正红门神道 2
Spirit Path of Front Red Gate 2

SPIRIT PATH

There are three straight flagstone pavements leading to the mausoleum after entering Front Red Gate. And the path right in front of Gate of Spirit is called Spirit Path, which is supposed to be used by spirits of tomb owners. Spirit Path starts from Front Red Gate and ends in front of Screen Wall of Crescent City at the back of the mausoleum, and this Path is regarded as the central axis of the mausoleum. The main buildings of the mausoleum are built on the central axis and other annex buildings are located along its both sides. According to mausoleum system of Qing Dynasty, the part between Great Red Gate and Eminent Favor Gate should be partitioned by another building, implying never-ending fengshui. In the eyes of ancient Chinese people, the thought of fengshui for ancestor tomb exerted direct and profound impact upon the lasting of imperial ruling. Therefore, there usually are Gable Screen Wall or Dragon-phoenix Gate built on Spirit Path to protect fengshui. There is no Gable Screen Wall on Spirit Path in Zhaoling Imperial Tomb, but a Stele Pavilion of Divine Merits is built to ensure the eternity of fengshui. Just like Gate of Spirit, Spirit Path was deemed inviolable. People couldn't walk along it anytime except on occasions of great sacrifices in Zhaoling Imperial Tomb. And even on these occasions nobody but the soldiers carrying sacrifices and blessing-praying plates could walk along it. And it was stipulated in Qing Dynasty that "People walking across Spirit Path will be punished, people walking down it will be executed, and its hoofs will be chopped off if a horse walks on it," which was strictly observed and followed.

大清国盛京奉天府工部理事官商全约副理官格勒布
Ge Lebu, Deputy Director of Mukden Ministry of Works in Qing Dynasty

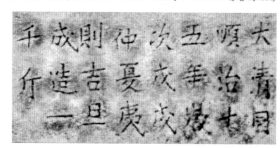

大清国顺治十五年岁次戊戌仲夏夷则吉旦成造一千斤
One-thousand-jin Bell Casted on Mid-summer of July 1 (Lunar Calendar) in the Fifteenth Ruling Year of Emperor Shunzhi (1658) in Qing Dynasty

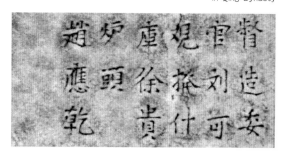

督造委官刘可观抵什库徐贵炉头赵应乾
Supervised by Liu Keguan, Checked by Xu Gui and Casted by Zhao Yingqian

东西红门

红墙内部是陵寝的风水中心，因此，也有风水红墙的说法。红墙，墙裙墙顶用黄色琉璃瓦构件装饰，墙的高度不同，东西两侧的红墙中间分别开有一门，称东红门和西红门。东西红门都是单间拱形洞门，形制与正红门相似，两侧也有蟠龙袖壁，只是颜色一黑，一绿，雕工同样精彩绝伦。

东西红门的使用也有严格的规定，在清代，东西红门是守陵官兵及进陵内打扫的夫役们走的门。东西红门的级别在规定上远远低于正红门。而事实上，像任何规定都有特例一样，在陵门的使用上也有特殊的情况。有记载，清代皇帝东巡前来祭祀昭陵时并不走正面大红门，而是走级别颇低的东西红门。

原来在东红门附近还建有钟亭，里面悬挂着一口高 1.24 米、口径 1.10 米、重达千斤的山陵钟。此钟铸造于顺治十五年（1658 年），是昭陵举行大祭和小祭敲击的"祭钟"。钟顶为双螭吊纽，钟体有行龙、花卉、八卦等纹饰，并铸有工部理事官、铸造官等人姓氏。相传，每至祭日正午均要鸣钟，此所谓"钟鸣鼎食"。民国之后，此钟又作为传报火警的用具。清朝末年，钟楼因年久失修不存在了，只有铁钟完好无损。现在作为文物，存放于仪仗房内。

东红门山陵钟及铭文／左图
Mausoleum Bell and Epigraph of East Red Gate／Left
东红门／右页图
East Red Gate／Right Page

EAST AND WEST RED GATES

Section of the mausoleum inside Red Wall is deemed as source of good fengshui, and therefore Red Wall is also known as Fengshui Wall. The red wall is decorated with glazed yellow tiles in its dado and crown, and it has different heights along with lay of the land. East and West Red Gates flank in the east and west part of Red Wall. The two Red Gates are of single arched portal in structure, similar to Front Red Gate. There are also curled-up dragon sleeve walls on either side of the two Gates, one wall in black, the other in green, which exhibit incomparable excellent carvings.

People passing East or West Red Gate should follow strict rules, and the two gates were for tomb guards and servants in Qing Dynasty. So East or West Red Gate was far more inferior in rank than Front Red Gate. But exception concerning the use of the gates is permissible like anything else. For example, according to historical records, emperors of Qing Dynasty passed East or West Red Gate rather than Front Red Gate when they offered sacrifices in Zhaoling Imperial Tomb during their inspection trips in the east.

There was a Bell Pavilion near East Red Gate. The bell inside is 1.24 meter high and 1.10 meter in diameter, weighing over 1,000 jin (one jin is half a kilogram). It was cast in the 15th reigning year of Emperor Shunzhi (1658) and used to toll during great and small sacrifices. The yoke on the bell crown is decorated with two li (legendary dragons without horns in ancient times) and the body has been inscribed with auspicious patterns such as flying dragons, flowers and Eight Diagrams (eight combinations of three whole or broken lines formerly used

in divination). Name of casters and the officials in charge can also be found on the bell. It is said that the bell would be tolled at noon of sacrifice. During the period of Republic of China, the bell was used to give warning of a fire. At the end of Qing Dynasty, the Bell Pavilion collapsed for being long neglected and in disrepair, but the bell remains intact, which is now kept in Honor Guards House as a cultural relic.

西红门 / 上图
West Red Gate / Upper

西红门旧照 / 右下图
Old Picture of West Red Gate / Lower Right

西红门袖壁 / 左下图
Sleeve Wall of West Red Gate / Lower Left

昭陵石象生掩映在神路两侧的松林里／左图
Stone Animal Statues Hidden in the Pines along Spirit Path in Zhaoling Imprial Tomb / Left
石象生石狮／上图
Stone Lion Statue / Upper

石象生花纹数量之谜

站在正红门下，面向北，正前方是一条笔直的南北走向的"神道"，神道两侧由南向北依次对称排放着一对石狮子，一对石獬豸（注解9），一对石麒麟，一对石马，一对石骆驼和一对石象。

在古时，神道被认为至高无上，是神灵通行的专属通道，不是活着的人可以随便走的。目无章法的人一旦肆意妄为，侮辱神明，就会受到惩罚。当时就有一种"横走罚，竖走杀，马过砍蹄"的惩罚说法。今天，在很多关于清代的电视剧中，我们都可以看到皇帝在两陵祭祖的镜头，其中，皇帝总是气宇轩昂、威风凛凛，甚至是大摇大摆地走在了正中的神道上。而君道和臣道上，也依次站满了身着朝服的大臣。每当看到这种场面，我都想，这不仅是人们关于历史的无知，也是因为想当然而犯的错误。可能除了研究历史的人，很少有人会去思考，

石象生麒麟／左页图
Stone Kilin Statue / Left Page
清东陵（孝陵）石象生麒麟／下图
Stone Kylin Statue of East Qing Mausoleum (Xiao Mausoleum) / Lower

甚至微微想一想，这三条同样细长的小道，究竟是做什么的，是简单的装饰还是别有用意？

在我们小的时候，昭陵里的这些石象生可是我们这群不懂事的孩子眼中极有乐趣的玩具之一。我还清晰地记得那样的画面，每年我们祭扫烈士陵园后，都会顺便跑到这来玩儿，骑在这些石象上面洋洋得意，十几个石象上爬满了小孩。直到现在每次站在石象生前面，我都会回忆起儿时的情景。

乾隆时期，乾隆帝命人在每一个石象生下面都加了汉白玉底座。从这些石象的材质推断，我猜想那对汉白玉制成的石马和石象，也应该是乾隆时期在加汉白玉底座时补造的。整体来看，石象生的排列是有规律的，由南向北，越往北石象生的体积越大。关于石象生须弥座花纹，东侧花纹都是有规律的对称，而西侧则略有差异。

石象生底座上的花纹，基本有两种形状，有的花瓣均匀，有的则由一大一小花瓣间隔组成。这让我想起，申遗时某著名学府的测绘图纸上，把石象生的底座花纹和数量全部画成了一样的，看来并不十分精确。

我又仔细数了数石象生底座上的花纹，发现狮子、獬豸、麒麟底座花纹个数比较对称。东侧须弥座南北花纹个数均为八个，西侧石象生则为九个。

立马须弥座花纹个数也是对称的，不同的是，东侧的立马须弥座花纹个数是十个，西侧却是九个。

东侧骆驼须弥座花纹个数是十一个，仍然比较对称，而西侧骆驼底座花纹则开始出现了差异，南面花纹个数十个，北面花纹个数十二个。

石象须弥座花纹，东侧南北都是十个，西侧石象须弥座南面九个，北面十个。我想，出现这种差异的可能就是，某个工人在雕刻的时候，要么偷懒了，要么就是技术不到位吧。

石象生作为护陵神兽，有特别的意义。比如，石象按古时的说法是取"太平有象"之意，希望保佑大清国事太平，国运兴隆。这对石马就更有故事了，它们的名字分别为"大白"、"小白"。传说皇太极生前有两匹心爱的坐骑，戎马倥偬的一世英雄在晚年对这两匹马爱护有加，不知道是不是对自己金戈铁马生涯的无限怀念，于是在皇太极死后，石匠就依据这两匹坐骑的样子雕刻了这两座石马，希望这位旷世奇主的英雄梦还能继续。

福陵中的石象生数目也是八个，可显然没有昭陵气派。我想，这可能和古代社会森严的等级礼制有关。努尔哈赤虽为皇太极的父亲，但是他最终还只是"大汗"，而皇太极才是大清朝第一位称为"皇帝"的人。还有一点和福陵不同的是，昭陵的东、西红门横穿过石象生，离安葬灵柩的地方比较远，福陵的东西红门比较近。关内的石象生，属清东陵孝陵的规模最大，共有十八对，而泰陵雍正时因为风水的问题曾不设置石象生，后来到乾隆十三年（1748年），乾隆帝为了彰显对祖先的孝道又恢复了设置，其间还引起了他与臣工抵牾的波折。其实乾隆皇帝一直想给自己的陵寝修石象生，但是因为他父亲雍正帝陵寝中没有石象生，所以他就想出了补建的办法，不仅如此，关外三陵中的很多石象生底座也是乾隆皇帝给补加的。关外石象生，虽然在石材上不如关内，但是在雕刻技法上却更加生动逼真，看起来像真的一样。关内的石象生，则更强调皇权与威严，多了文臣武将的石象，动物都是卑躬屈膝的，如跪着的大象等，不得不佩服古人，将至高无上演绎到如此程度。

RIDDLE OF NUMBER OF DECORATIVE PATTERN ON STONE ANIMAL STATUES

A south-north direction Spirit Path comes into your sight if you stand below Front Red Gate, facing north. There are, on both sides of Spirit Path and from south to north, a pair of stone lions, a pair of stone xie zhis (see Note 9), a pair of stone kylins, a pair of stone horses, a pair of stone camels and a pair of stone elephants arranged in symmetry.

In ancient times, Spirit Path was deemed sacred as the exclusive passage for spirits, and no living souls could walk upon it randomly. Anyone who disobeyed this rule would be considered insulting the divinity and thus incurred fearful punishment. It was said at that time that "People walking across Spirit Path will be punished, people walking down it will be executed, and its hoofs will be chopped off if a horse walks on it." And in many teleplays today about Qing Dynasty, audience may see something of an emperor prancing through the middle Spirit Path with great dignity when they offered sacrifices to their ancestors, with his court officials following behind on Path of Emperor or Officials, dressed in court dress. Whenever I see such a scene, a thought will occur to me that such things would be impossible in history and such kind of plays reflect their ignorance of historical facts. Apart from people studying history, few will even take the slightest consideration of what the three paths are used for: for pure ornament or something else?

And when I was young, these stone animal statues were only funny toys for us because we knew little about these respectable sculptures. And recollection of that time is still vivid in my mind. When we visited and swept the memorial park, children of my age would mount the stone animal statues and had fun there, and sometimes all the statues had jaunty children playing on them. Childhood memories can still pop up whenever I stand in front of these statues.

During the reign of Emperor Qianlong, he issued an imperial order to put white marble bases under those stone animal statues. Judging from their material, I inferred that the stone horses and elephants made out of white marble were probably sculptured at that time. On the whole, those statues are arranged in a regular way: the size of the sculptured animals becomes larger one after another from south to north. Decorative patterns of their Sumeru bases on the east-side are in orderly symmetry while those on the west side differ slightly.

The decorative patterns on the Sumeru bases basically fall into two forms: even pedals, and uneven pedals with one big and one small altenatively. I remembered that when Zhaoling Imperial Tomb applied to be recognized as World Heritage, all the patterns and their numbers of the stone animals were the same on the survey drawings, which is indeed inaccurate.

I counted the decorative patterns of these stone animal statues and found the number of patterns on the bases of stone lions, xie zhis and kylins are symmetrical. The numbers of decorative patterns on both south and north of the east-side Sumeru base are all eight while the number of the east-side Sumeru base is nine.

The number of decorative patterns on the Sumeru base of stone horse is also symmetrical. But their numbers are different, with 10 on the east-side Sumeru base and 9 on the west-side one.

The east-side stone camel has 11 flower patterns on its Sumeru base, which are still symmetrical both in its south part and north part, but the west-side stone camel has 10 flower patterns in its south part of Sumeru base and 12 in its north part.

The east-side stone elephant has 10 flower patterns on its Sumeru base both in its south part and north part while the west-side stone elephant has 9 in its

south part and 10 in its north. In my opinion, the differences in decorative patterns of these stone animals resulted from negligence or lack of technique.

As mythical divine guards of protecting mausoleums, stone elephant implies peace and prosperity according to ancient Chinese culture. Elephant statues are thus placed here in hopes of praying for blessings from heaven, protecting Qing Dynasty and ensuring its peace, thriving prosperity. The pair of stone horses here have more interesting origin, who are named as Da Bai (Big White Horse) and Xiao Bai (Little White Horse) respectively. It was said that Hong Taiji had two beloved saddle horses, which he treasured very much in his senior years after he had been engaged in warfare all his lifetime, and the two horses thus become a reminder of his experience of shining spears and armored horses. So after death of Hong Taiji, two stone horse statues were carved imitating the live ones, hoping this outstanding emperor could still enjoy the company of his beloved horses.

Fu Mausoleum also has 8 stone animal statues, which obviously couldn't match the magnificence of those in Zhaoling Imperial Tomb. In my opinion, the difference reveals the strict hierarchical social order of ancient China. Nurhaci was father of Hong Taiji, but he was only titled as Khan of Manchu, while

清东陵（孝陵）石象生骆驼／上图
Stone Camel Statue of East Qing Mausoleum (Xiao Mausoleum) / Upper

昭陵石象生骆驼／右页图
Stone Camel Statue of Zhaoling Imperial Tomb / Right Lage

石象生立象／左图
Stone Elephant Statue / Left
清东陵（孝陵）石象生卧象／上图
Crouching Elephant Statue of East Qing Mausoleum (Xiao Mausoleum)/ Upper

Hong Taiji was the first emperor of Qing Dynasty. Another distinction between Zhao and Fu Mausoleum also indicates hierarchical difference of their tomb owners in that East or West Red Gate of Zhaoling Imperial Tomb extending across the stone animals is far from inner tomb while East or West Red Gate of Fu Mausoleum is nearer. As for the stone animal statues outside the Shanhai Pass, Xiao Mausoleum has the largest scale, with 18 pairs in all. There aren't such statues in Tai Mausoleum of Emperor Yongzheng due to certain geomantic reasons. But later in the 13th ruling year (1748) of Emperor Qianlong, he restored the construction of stone animal statues, which had caused contradictory anecdotes between Emperor and his officials. In fact, Emperor Qianlong wanted to build the statues in his own mausoleum, but there were no statues in his father's mausoleum. So he came up with the idea to restore stone animal statues in his father Yongzheng's Mausoleum. He also added bases to many statues in Three Mausoleums outside Shanhai Pass. Although materials used for those statues are not as good as those inside Shanhai Pass, their carving technique are more vivid, which help make the statues look like real animals. However, the statues inside the Pass lay more emphasis on imperial power and majesty, in which kneeling animals such as elephants, together with the obsequious officials, illustrate the supreme power to the unprecedented level.

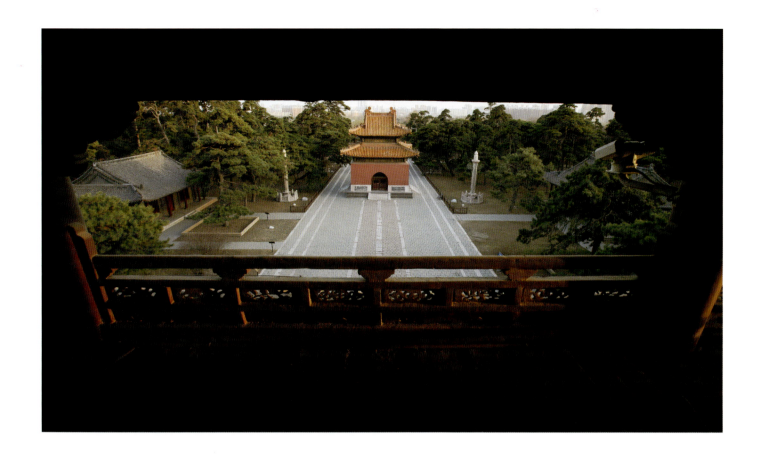

不是所有清帝都能立神功圣德碑

神道的尽头就是大碑楼了。昭陵神功圣德碑立在大碑楼正中，正面写着"大清昭陵神功圣德碑"九个遒劲大字，后面是洋洋洒洒的几千字，书写着皇太极戎马一生的功德，可以说神功圣德碑就是皇帝一生的功劳簿。

从可以查阅的资料来看，立神功圣德碑的礼制开始于大约六百年以前，第一块圣德碑是朱棣为其父亲朱元璋立的，立于明孝陵的方城之内，用以歌颂明太祖的功德。由此估计，一直沿袭至清朝。但清朝自道光皇帝开始，之后五位皇帝的陵寝都没有神功圣德碑。原因是1842年中英签订了丧权辱国的《南京条约》，鸦片战争失败，中国从此陷入了深重的灾难之中，道光帝自觉"愧对祖宗"、"愧对天下百姓"，于是下旨取消了在皇陵内立歌功颂德的神功圣德碑和石象生。关外三陵中，昭陵、福陵都各自只有一块神功圣德碑，永陵里却有四块神功圣德碑，成了真帝最少、碑楼最多的清代陵寝。纵观清朝历史，功绩最大的皇帝，大家可能都会想到康熙皇帝。而不仅是我们这样认为，古人也这样认为，所以，神功圣德碑亭内立着双碑以彰显这位皇帝的功劳，从此成为定制。因此，雍正帝、乾隆帝、嘉庆帝陵寝的神功圣德碑也都是两块，才形成了这样几位皇帝的神功圣德碑都是双碑的特殊情形，直到道光帝，这种情况才有所变化。清代皇帝中道光帝没有立神功圣德碑，因为清朝祖制中规定，"凡后世皇帝失国土尺地寸土者，不得立神功圣德碑"。其实历数各朝各代，清朝是出明君最多的朝代，清12位皇帝，每位都很勤勉，可惜到了清末，西方列强的发展远远超过了清朝，在强大的铜炮火枪面前，长矛和大刀，是根本无法取胜的。

帝王的皇陵，向来不缺少的就是似无还有的诡异传说，关于神功圣德碑就有一个。流传出的故事是说，每当阴雨天气，圣德碑上面会隐约显现出人的形状，身材修颀、飘洒如仙，极像一个面容姣好的曼妙女郎。而且，话说越仔细揣摩，这个人形就越加清晰。这种说法慢慢传开，吸引了不少文人达官等着雨天来到昭陵一看究竟，还得了"神碑幻影"的美名。去的人多了，说法也就随着多了起来，和这有关的故事也就越来越玄。当然也有人从科学的角度解释过这种现象出现的合理性。无论最终的原因究竟是怎样的，我想对于我们普通百姓而言，这些故事都让我们觉得昭陵有着看不透的神秘，让我们对那里更加向往，这也就足够了。

碑楼
Stele Pavilion

清东陵（孝陵）神功圣德碑楼 / 上图
Stele Pavilion of Divine Merits of East Qing Mausoleum (Xiao Mausoleum) / Upper
清末祭祀旧照 / 下图
Old Picture of Sacrificial Ceremony in the Late Qing Dynasty / Lower
昭陵大碑楼 / 右图
Great Stele Pavilion of Zhaoling Imperial Tomb / Right

GREAT STELE PAVILION OF DIVINE MERITS, NOT ERECTED FOR ALL EMPERORS

Great Stele Pavilion is right at the end of Spirit Path. Stele of Divine Merits of Zhaoling Imperial Tomb is erected in the very center of the Pavilion, upon which are inscribed nine vigorous Chinese characters "Da Qing Zhao Ling Shen Gong Sheng De Bai" (meaning Stele of Divine Merits of Zhaoling Imperial Tomb of Great Qing Dynasty). Under the inscription is a detailed account of Hong Taiji's deeds – his military life and divine achievements. It is safe to conclude that a Stele of Divine Merits is a recording of an emperor's lifetime feats.

From available records, we can see that the practice of erecting steles of divine merits started from approximately six hundred years ago, and the first stele of its kind was set up by Emperor Zhu Di of Ming Dynasty for his father, Emperor Zhu Yuanzhang (First Emperor of Ming Dynasty) inside Square City of Ming Xiao Mausoleum, in praise of the merits and virtues of the founding emperor. And then such convention is followed and practiced till Qing Dynasty. But no Stele of Divine Merits had been built from Emperor Daoguang. After the defeat of Opium War, Treaty of Nanking was signed in 1842, which surrendered China's sovereign rights under humiliating terms, throwing China into disasters. Emperor Daoguang considered himself guilty of smirching the great fame of his forefathers and felt remorse and shame for his subjects, thus annulling the building

清西陵（慕陵）隆恩殿外四棱石幢 / 上图
Four-arris Stone Stele outside Eminent Favor Hall in West Qing Mausoleum (Mu Mausoleum) / Upper

神功圣德碑 / 左图
Stele of Divine Merits / Left

of Steles of Divine Merits and stone animal statues inside his imperial mausoleum. Among Three Mausoleums outside Shanhai Pass, Zhaoling Imperial Tomb and Fu Mausoleum each have one Stele of Divine Merits while Yong Mausoleum has four, making itself a Mausoleum in Qing Dynasty with least emperors and most steles. Throughout the history of Qing Dynasty, the emperor with the greatest achievements should be Emperor Kangxi. Not only we think so but also our ancestors did. So the two steles inside Great Stele Pavilion of Divine Merits highlight the emperor's divine merits, and since then it became a tradition to set up steles of divine merits. Therefore, there are also two steles of divine merits in the mausoleums of emperors Yongzheng, Qianlong and Jiaqing, but from Emperor Daoguang, this tradition began to change. No stele of divine merits was set up for Emperor Daoguang, as it was regulated in the ancient system of Qing Dynasty, "Any future emperor shall not deserve steles of divine merits if he loses one inch of land." Actually, there are 12 emperors in Qing Dynasty, which is a dynasty full of most sagacious emperors, and all of the emperors were assiduous. Pitifully, at the end of Qing Dynasty, the western powers surpassed Qing Dynasty with a large gap. Compared with cannons and muskets, there wasn't any chance for spears and broadswords to win.

Secretive folk legends always loom inside and around imperial mausoleums. Stele of Divine Merits of Zhaoling Imperial Tomb is no exception. The prevailing tale goes like this: an indistinct slender and swaying figure would emerge above the stele whenever it was cloudy or rainy. The figure resembled exactly a good-looking fair lady, and the more you gazed at it, the more distinct the figure looked like a real human. The tale spread so widely that many men of letters and prominent officials and eminent personages came for a visit with admiration. Stele of Divine Merits was therefore beautifully dubbed as "Divine stele with illusory beauty." As more people visited the place, various versions of the tale came into existence, and some of them were more incredible. Of course, some even tried to interpret the phenomenon from the perspective of science. However, no matter what might lie behind the myth, these tales only fortify the unconceivable mystical nature of Zhaoling Imperial Tomb, which makes it more attractive for ordinary people. And that's what really counts.

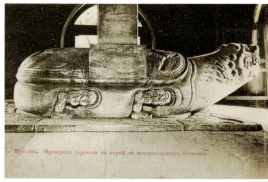

神功圣德碑／左页图
Stele of Divine Merits / Left Page
神功圣德碑老照片／左上图
Old Picture of Stele of Divine Merits / Upper Left
神功圣德碑基座四角图案／左下图
Patterns at Four Corners of the Base of Stele of Divine Merits / Lower Left
神功圣德碑拓片／右图
Rubbing of Stele of Divine Merits / Right

茶膳房
Catering House

昭陵祭祀

在神功圣德碑后与隆恩门之间，东西有两个建筑群。东西看似对称，昭陵西边有两处建筑已经不存在了。而这些都是当年专门为祭祀作准备的地方。作为陵寝文化的顶峰代表，清代的祭祀，我也专门研究过。清陵祭祀不仅礼节繁缛，而且等级极为森严。每次昭陵祭祀，都需要长期的准备，而每当皇帝亲临，场面就更加盛大了。因为盛京是清朝的开国都城，既是龙兴之地，又为祖宗陵寝之所在，因而清帝在入主中原后，对这一祖宗发祥重地给予了特殊的关照。自康熙十年(1671年)始，圣祖玄烨继承父志来到盛京，祭祀了坐落在盛京的祖宗陵寝，从而开创了清帝"东巡祭祖"的定制。历朝皇家都把上陵礼、皇陵祭祀作为推崇皇权、维护统治的一种重要形式和手段，而清朝则把它发挥到极致。守陵人也由最初的12人发展到进关后的总管衙门和掌官防两衙门执行管理，形成了一套专门的管理机构。每当祭祀，所有大事小事，具体到抬供桌的官员名单的确认，都要经过公文级级呈报，繁琐而严格。

清朝按祭祀种类规模大致可分为大祭、小祭和特祭。大祭每年举行两次，皇帝和皇后的忌日，其中，清明、中元、冬至、岁暮又称"四时大祭"，是祭祀中等级最高、礼制最繁琐、祭品最丰盛的祭祀形式。清明大祭中最有特色的是"敷土礼"，即是往宝顶上添土，这与民间培土修坟的习俗相似。小祭，又叫"常祭"、"朔望祭"，包括每月的朔望即初一、十五；小祭比大祭无论就祭祀规模还是承祭官的品级等方面都低。除以上祭祀外，还包括特祭，就是指因国家大典而在昭陵临时举行的告祭礼，如每年皇帝或皇太后生日举行的"万寿告祭"，为皇太后加徽号举行的告祭，或出征凯旋向陵告祭，或皇子每隔三年来此行礼。当然场面最隆重的还是皇帝亲临祭祖。

对比一下当年的昭陵照片，发现祭祀用的饽饽房、果房等都是有烟囱的，而现在我拍摄的照片上，饽饽房、果房等房子上的烟囱都不知哪去了。烟囱在满族建筑中是重要的一种特色，尤其是在陵寝祭祀中，无论是饽饽房还是茶膳房，都是需要生火的，烟囱起着排烟的作用，而现在没有了烟囱的饽饽房和茶膳房，不仅失去了当年祭祀中的实际功能，也影响了满族建筑风格特色。在沈阳故宫中，甚至还可以看见一座高耸的烟囱，谓之"一统天下"，可见满族人对烟囱这一建筑的重视。而在皇陵中，也

同样给烟囱留了位置，只是百年建筑历经风雨，不断破损与不断修葺，不知道什么时候、什么人，竟自作主张将这看似已经无用的烟囱修没了，抑或是遗忘了。保护文物与修复文物都主张"修旧如旧"，希望以后有机会，能够还原文物的原貌吧。同样的清代陵寝，关内的清东陵和清西陵中仍然可见楼顶上的烟囱，而关外三陵的文物保护工作，难免令人堪忧。

ZHAOLING IMPERIAL TOMB SACRIFICES

There are two building complexes between the back of Stele Pavilion of Divine Merits and Eminent Favor Gate. The two building complexes are seemingly symmetrical, and it's hard to tell as two buildings on the west side are gone. All these buildings were specially built for sacrificial ceremonies of Zhaoling Imperial Tomb. I have made a special study over the funeral culture of the Qing Dynasty mausoleums, which represent the acme of China's funeral culture. The etiquette of mausoleum sacrifice was strict and should be well prepared. Especially when the Emperor arrived, the scene was more than grand. For Shengjing is the founding capital of Qing Dynasty and cemetery of their ancestors, Qing emperors all pay their special attention to this cradle land of their ancestors after they dominated the Central Plains of China. In the 10th year of Emperor Kangxi (1671), following his father's footsteps, Hiowan Yei came to Shengjing to offer sacrifices to their ancestral mausoleum. Since then, the system of "East Tour for Ancestor Worship" was established. Emperors of every dynasty all took the sacrificial system as an important form and measure to consolidate their ruling. In Qing Dynasty, mausoleum etiquette and ritual of sacrificial offering came to the acme. The mausoleum guards also outgrew the original 12 guards to a complete administrative system. All sacrificial details, even including the name list of the officials carrying sacrificial boards should be reported and approved, following strict control and management.

According to sacrificial scale of Qing Dynasty, sacrificial offerings can be divided into grand, small and special. Grand sacrifices were held twice a year on the death anniversary of Emperor or Empress. In addition, Tomb sweeping Festival, Ghost Festival, Winter Solstice, close of the year are also called as "Grand sacrifices in four seasons," with the highest level, the most complicated rites and most sumptuous offerings in all the sacrifices. "Hilling-up Rite" is the most featured grand sacrifice in Qingming Festival, which is to add soil on top of the grave, similar to the civil custom of tomb reheaping. Small-sized sacrifice, also called "Regular sacrifice" or "Lunar sacrifice," much smaller than Grand sacrifice in terms of size and lower in rank of host officer, took place on the 1st day and 15th day of each month. In addition to the above-said sacrifices, there is special sacrifice, which is a temporal rite due to national ceremonies held in Fu Mausoleum, such as "Boundless Longevity Announcement Sacrifice" for birthdays of Emperor or Empress dowager, Announcement Sacrifice awarding emblems for Empress dowager, Announcement Sacrifice before and after a war, or courtesy paid by princes every three years. Undoubtedly, the emperor's sacrificial offering ceremony was the grandest.

When I once compared the photos I took a long time ago with recent ones, I found that chimneys of Bo Bo Fang (Pastry House) and Fruit House were all gone. Chimneys are an important feature in Manchu architecture. It is especially true for both Pastry House and Tea and Food House during mausoleum sacrifices because fire is needed

仪仗房、果房旧照，房上还有烟筒／左上图
Old Picture of Honor Guards House and Fruit House (still with chimney) / Upper Left
修缮后的仪仗房、果房，房上烟筒消失了／左下图
Renovated Honor Guards House and Fruit House (with chimney disappeared) / Lower Left
茶膳房／右图
Catering House / Right
仪仗房后的楼旧照，现已不存在／右页图
Old Picture of a building behind Honor Guards House (no longer exist) / Right Page

方城／左图
Square City / Left
向内倾斜的马道／下图
Intilted Horse Track / Lower

and chimneys function as smoke extractors. But the present Pastry House and Tea and Food House with no chimneys lead to both the loss of its original functions of sacrifices and the changes of Manchu architectural features. There is a tall chimney even in Imperial Palace of Shenyang, implying the unification of the whole world, from which we can see how much Manchu people value chimneys. In mausoleums of emperors, there was room made for chimneys. Through a century's process of damage and repair, we have no idea when and who made his own mind to repair the seemingly useless chimney into nothing. Or maybe the chimney was forgotten? Protecting and renovating cultural relics should follow the principle of "repairing as it were." I think it will be better if these chimneys can be restored to their original appearance. Of all the mausoleums of Qing Dynasty, the chimneys of East or West Qing Mausoleums inside Shanhai Pass are well protected, while the protection of Three Mausoleums outside the Pass is a little worrying.

清代帝陵独有的方城

碑楼之北是方城，昭陵方城城墙都是青砖垒砌，顺着略微陡峭的楼梯，可以走到方城上面，方城上有马道，也都是青砖铺砌，路面微微向内倾斜，这也正是古代建筑设计者的智慧所在，所谓"肥水不外流"，每当雨雪天气，积水就会顺势流下，不过让人费解的是，这么大的城排水是怎么解决的呢？

我仔细观察过昭陵的排水系统，发现在宝顶周围向内倾斜度度更大，水全流向宝顶，宝顶周围还有入水孔，而与此矛盾的是地宫最需要做的就是防水，那这么大量的水都流向哪里呢？这真是一个谜。在方城架设监控设施的时候，曾经挖开过宝城与方城的下水道……仅此一点，就让我常常感慨，古人匠心。而古人这样的哲学思想背后需要有多大的科技力量的支持啊！

关外三陵中，永陵是没有方城的，只有很矮的墙，甚至没有隆恩门、隆恩殿，而是启运门和启运殿。比较昭陵与福陵方城，昭陵方城比福陵方城的墙高2.7米，比较两陵方城大小，昭陵方城东西城墙与配殿有10.06米的距离，几乎是福陵的4倍，而福陵东西城墙几乎贴到了东西配殿的殿角。而昭陵内有五座大型建筑，福陵内只有三座大型建筑，规模上昭陵更显雍容大度。这和大清江山已经日渐稳固是有必然联系的。关于昭陵内的五座建筑，我依然认为，这和沈阳故宫的台上五宫是异曲同工的，都源于满族先人的居住习惯，喜欢在台上建城，比如赫图阿拉。只是故宫的台上五宫，是给人实际居住用的，而昭陵内的建筑是给灵魂象征性居住的，所以一般陵寝建筑的规制比正常人使用的要矮很多，小很多。比如隆恩门，从地面到楼顶三层通高才21.92米。尽管如此，帝王们还是给先祖和自己都建了方城这样一个类似真正城堡的陵寝，是希望在另一个世界里依然可以称王称帝，帝业永存吧。

清代陵寝，关内陵寝一般都没有方城，道光帝的慕陵甚至没有宝城，关外三陵相比，昭陵与福陵类似，昭陵方城内有五处大型建筑。尽管孝陵也有一处与关外清陵同名为方城的建筑，却是同名不同概念。关外的方城是相对于月牙城而言的，不是单指形状上是方的就叫方城的，关外的方城都是类似真正的城，里面包含隆恩殿、东西配殿等大型建筑。孝陵的方城却是类似于关外月牙城部分，里面只包含影壁墙和登城台阶，没有实质性建筑，两者除了名字一样，几乎在形制与功能上完全不同。可以说，方城是关外清陵独有的，也是清代帝王陵寝独有的建筑。

从东北角楼望方城马道
Horse Track of Square City, Seen from Northeast Turret

SQUARE CITY, WHICH ONLY MAUSOLEUMS OF QING DYNASTY POSSESS

Square City is right to the north of Stele Pavilion, whose walls are all built with grey bricks. People can ascend onto the top of Square City by walking along the slightly steep stairs. The horse tracks of Square City are also paved with grey bricks, a little tilted inward. Such design reveals wisdom of ancient architects, for it implies the meaning of "give your own fish-guts to your own sea-maws." In snowy or rainy weather, water will flow naturally down along the terrain. While looking at such a large building complex, I wonder how the drainage system works to prevent the mausoleum from floods.

After a careful study of the overall drainage system of Zhaoling Imperial Tomb, I find that the perimeter of Blessed Mound tilt inward with water inlets around. What contradicts with this design is that the underground palace needs to be protected from any possible water damage. So I wonder where the water flows after through these inlets, which is really a puzzle to be solved. The drainage tunnels had once been dug up under Blessed Mound and Square City when monitoring facilities were set up for Square City, which uniquely lead to my admiration of our ancestors for their philosophical wisdom in architectural design.

Among Three Mausoleums outside Shanhai Pass, Yong Mausoleum has no Square City but low wall around, and it has no Eminent Favor Gate and Hall, but Qiyun Gate and Hall (Luck-provoking Gate and Hall). Comparing Square Cities of the other two mausoleums, we find that the wall of Square City in Zhaoling Imperial Tomb is 2.7 meters higher than that of Fu Mausoleum, and the distance from East Wall to East Side-hall or from West Wall to West Side-hall is 10.06 meters, nearly four times of that in Fu Mausoleum. The walls in Square City nearly touch the turrets of its East or West Side-hall. There are three palaces inside Fu Mausoleum, but five in Zhaoling Imperial Tomb, looking more imperial and magnificent in scale, which is correlated with the consolidated reign of Qing Dynasty. The five buildings inside Zhaoling Imperial Tomb are of the same style with those in Mukden Palace, which are to match the customs of Ancient Manchu people, who were fond of building cities on top of platforms, like Hetuala. But differences lie in that the five palaces in-

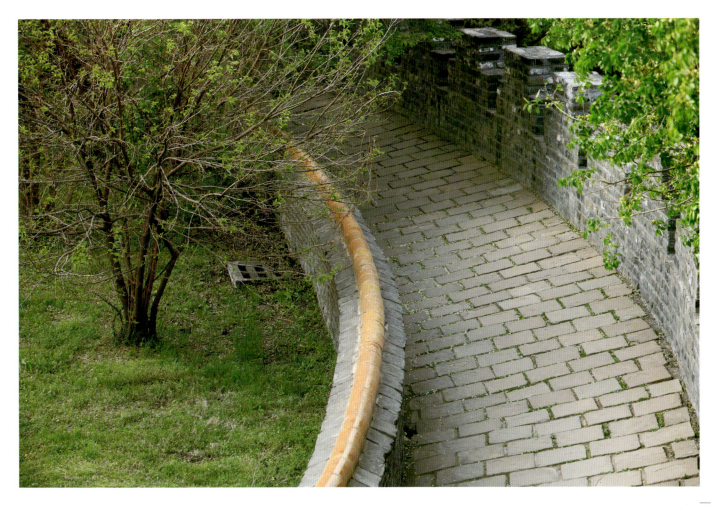

宝城马道／上图
Horse Track of Burial Bastion / Upper

西方城马道／下图
Horse Track of West Square City / Lower

side the Imperial Palace are for residence while those inside Zhaoling Imperial Tomb are symbolic habitats for souls. Therefore, mausoleum buildings are much lower and smaller than those for living people, like Eminent Favor Hall, which is only 21.92 meters from top to floor covering three stories altogether. Even so, the emperors still built castle-like mausoleums for their ancestors and themselves, in hopes of still ruling in another world like emperors even after they passed away.

Generally speaking, there are no Square Cities among Qing mausoleums inside Shanhai Pass. For example, there isn't even Burial Bastion inside Mu Mausoleum of Emperor Daoguang. But among Three Mausoleums outside Shanhai Pass, the same features are shared by Fu Mausoleum and Zhaoling Imperial Tomb, and there are five large buildings inside Square City of Zhaoling Imperial Tomb. Although there is a Square City inside Xiao Mausoleum, but this Square City is different from those outside Shanhai Pass. Square City outside the Pass is so called with comparison to Crescent City, and it not only refers to the square form but also they are real city walls, which include large buildings such as Eminent Favor Hall and East or West Side-hall. In contrast, Square City of Xiao Mausoleum is only like Crescent City, which includes gable screen wall and the stairs leading to the city wall. They are different in terms of forms and functions. It can be inferred that Square City is unique to Qing mausoleums outside Shanhai Pass, and it is mausoleum architecture only Qing Dynasty possess.

隆恩门门杠／上图
Latch of Eminent Favor Gate / Upper
隆恩门／右图
Eminent Favor Gate / Right

倒插的隆恩门

方城内有隆恩殿、东西配殿、东西晾果房和焚帛亭。而隆恩门正是方城的城门。

昭陵的隆恩门，门额上黑色字迹非常小，如此大气的建筑配着极不相称的小字，不知古人用意之所在。隆恩门顶部有门楼，俗称"五凤楼"，上面绘有绚丽的龙凤彩绘，皇家气派壮丽威严。站在隆恩门下的门洞里，阴风袭人，门洞里有两扇大门，门上同样有面兽及金色门钉，与福陵不同的是，昭陵隆恩门正反两面都有门钉，南面门钉每行8个，总计个数84个；北面门钉个数每行9个，总计120个，两面个数不同。还有长木门闩，门闩由外插上，使人不必留在里面。一般门洞门闩都是设在城内的，防止外人进入，隆恩门正与之相反，每当走到这儿，我都会想起东北人常说的"倒插门女婿"（注解10）。白天门闩就横放在门洞的墙角，如树一样粗壮的门闩，不知道究竟是防什么用的。不过，昭陵隆恩门内也是可以插上的，起到了双重防护的作用。与关内清陵相比，关内清陵都没有倒插的隆恩门。

隆恩门是整个昭陵最高的建筑，比福陵的还要高，据说从前天气晴好时，登楼远眺，甚至可以看见百里之外的辽阳太子河。隆恩门两侧的马道由青砖铺就而成，可以供行人上下。而且，由于经年历久，这马道已经被踩成了"U"形，路面由外向内倾斜。

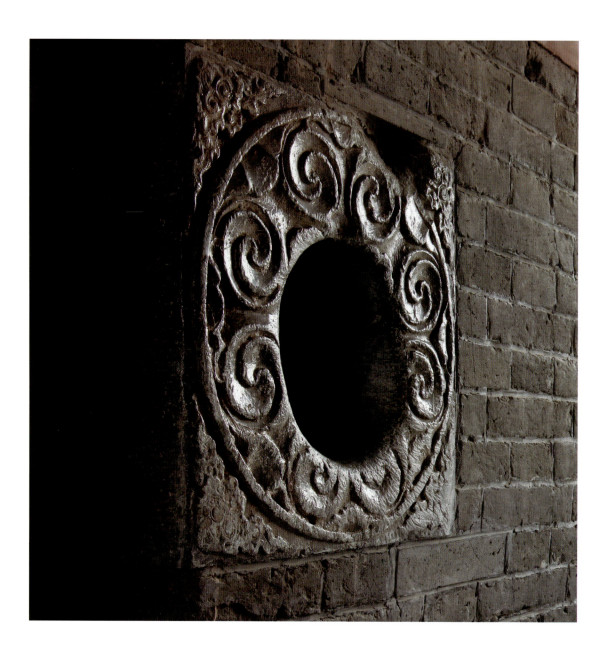

EMINENT FAVOR GATE, WHICH CAN BE LATCHED FROM OUTSIDE

Inside Square City are located such buildings as Eminent Favor Hall, East and West Side-halls, East and West Fruit Airing Houses and Silk-burning Pavilion. Eminent Favor Gate stands out as entrance of the City.

The sharp contrast of those tiny black characters above the lintel of Eminent Favor Gate against the magnificence of the building can be confusing: nobody knows the real intention of the ancient. On the top of Eminent Favor Gate is a gateway tower called "Five-phoenix Tower", painted with gorgeous colored dragon and phoenix drawings. These drawings are magnificent and stately, radiating imperial lustre. People standing in the archway under the Gate may feel gusts of cool breeze. There is a double-leaf door in the archway, on which animal heads and golden doornails can be found. The doors of Eminent Favor

隆恩门门杠石洞／上图
Latch Hole of Eminent Favor Gate / Upper
隆恩门鎏金兽头／右页图
Gilded Animal Head of Eminent Favor Gate / Right Page

夕照隆恩门／左页图
Eminent Favor Gate in Sunset / Left Page
日出隆恩门／上图
Eminent Favor Gate in Sunrise / Upper

Gate of Zhaoling Imperial Tomb are nailed on both sides, which is different from that of Fu Mausoleum. There are 8 nails in a line and 84 altogether on its south direction and 9 nails in a line, 120 altogether on its north. There is also a long wood latch to lock the door from outside. Door latches are usually used inside doors to prevent unwanted people from entering. Whenever I pass Eminent Favor Gate, the idea of a "married-in son-in-law" (See Note 10) may come into my mind. At daytime the lath as sturdy as a tree trunk will be laid in the corner of the archway. However, Eminent Favor Gate can also be latched from inside, ensuring that the building can be duly protected.

Eminent Favor Gate is the tallest part in the whole Zhaoling Imperial Tomb, even higher than that of Fu Mausoleum. It is said that on a sunny day, you can overlook River Taizi a hundred miles away in Liaoyang. The horse tracks along both sides of Eminent Favor Gate are paved with grey bricks, which is accessible to pedestrians. Due to years of wearing-out, the tracks have been treaded into a U-shape and their surface tilts inward from outside.

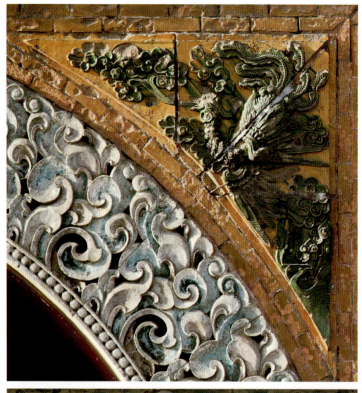

隆恩门龙凤琉璃砖雕、石雕／上图
Glazed Brick and Stone Carvings with Patterns of Dragon and Phoenix on Eminent Favor Gate / Upper

凤楼残月／右页图
Phoenix Tower under Waning Moon / Right Page

方城马道阶梯／上图
Stairs of Horse Track inside Square City ／ Upper
方城马道阶梯扶手上、下石狮／下图
Upper and Lower Stone Lions on Stair Rail of Horse Track ／ Lower
隆恩门内木楼梯／右页图
Wooden Stairs inside Eminent Favor Gate ／ Right Page

隆恩门沥粉贴金彩绘／左图、上一图、上二图
Embossed and Gilded Colored Painting of Eminent Favor Gate / Left, Upper First, Upper Second

清西陵（泰陵）隆恩门天花板／上三图
Ceiling of Eminent Favor Gate of West Qing Mausoleum (Tai Mausoleum) / Upper Third

隆恩门横剖面图／下图
Cross Section of Eminent Favor Gate / Lower

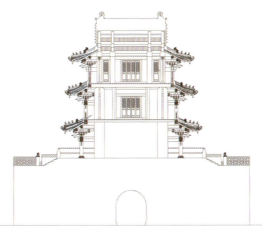

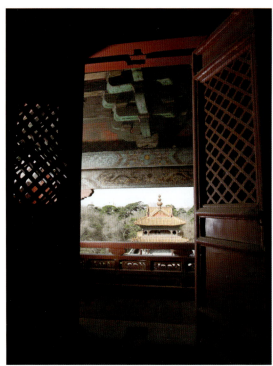

摄影的最佳视点——角楼

昭陵方城四隅各有角楼，显得异常雄伟。昭陵角楼雕梁画栋，雄伟之余也为昭陵增加了几许华贵。昭陵角楼均为两层结构，四座角楼均为重檐歇山式建筑，四面出廊，底层有拱门，楼内有木制楼梯通往二层，内外油饰彩画。角楼上有一宝葫芦，寓意"陵寝平平安安"。站在角楼上，可俯视整座陵寝，我经常站在角楼上拍摄昭陵全景，从摄影角度说，昭陵角楼是最有表现力的。特别是拍摄月牙城的时候，我腰上系着安全带，身体悬在角楼外，心想要有燕子李三的功夫就好了，拍摄就不用系安全带了。

在角楼的檐下悬有惊雀风铃，主要防止鸟雀栖息。昭陵角楼，继承了我国古代木构建筑灵活多变的传统做法，使用功能和装饰效果得以巧妙地结合，展示出我国古代匠师们的高超技艺和卓越才能。与福陵相比，昭陵角楼则保存完好，而福陵西北角楼坏损比较严重，永陵没有方城，更没有角楼。纵观清代帝王陵寝，关内清陵都没有方城，因此就没有角楼，而关外的方城都有角楼，只是这里的角楼几乎已经没有了防御功能，因为建筑比较矮，并不方便实际使用。而方城上还有楼梯蹬，可以直接从外面直接登上方城马道，关内的清陵一般都是内置楼梯，从内部上下的。

西南角楼／上图
Southwest Turret／Upper

西北角楼／右页图
Nothwest Turret／Right Page

TURRETS — IDEAL SPOT OF PHOTO-TAKING

Four turrets are built at the four corners of Square City, standing there spectacularly. Their carved beams and painted rafters also add some nobleness to these buildings. Turrets are two-storyed buildings with multi-eave gable and hip roof, of which there are corridors in all four sides and arched doors on the first floor, and inside there are wooden stairs leading to the second floor with painted drawings. On the top of the turrets is a Magic Gourd, which implies meaning of peace and safety. Standing on the turrets, one can overlook the entire mausoleum. I often stand here to shoot panoramas of Fu Mausoleum. From perspective of photography, corner turrets are most expressive. In particular, when I shot Crescent City, I was then hanging outside the turrets with my waist fastened with safety belt. I am always thinking if I know Kungfu like Swallow Li San, it's unnecessary to fasten safety belt.

There are iron-wrought bird-driving wind bells swinging under four corners of the turret cornices to scare away birds in case they nest here. The Turrets inherited the flexible craftsmanship of traditional wooden architecture of China, combining perfectly function of use and decorative effect and exhibiting the excellent skill and great aptitude of ancient craftsmen. Turrets of Zhaoling Imperial Tomb are better preserved, in contrast, the northwest turret of Fu Mausoleum is seriously damaged while Yong Mausoleum has neither Square City nor turret. Of all the mausoleums of Qing Dynasty, there are no Square Cities inside Shanhai Pass, let alone turrets. While there are turrets in Square Cities of the mausoleums outside Shanhai Pass, their defense function is almost lost, as it is not practical for use due to its relatively low buildings. In addition, there are stairs on Square City, which directly lead to the horse tracks of the City from outside the City. The mausoleums of Qing Dynasty inside the Pass are generally equipped with built-in stairs for access from inside.

东北角楼／上图
Northeast Turret / Upper
西北角楼／右页图
Nothwest Turret / Right Page

隆恩殿 / 左图
Eminent Favor Hall / Left
隆恩殿旧照 / 上图
Old Picture of Eminent Favor Hall / Upper

为太宗帝后灵魂居住的隆恩殿

如果说昭陵的建筑各有特色，犹如天空中璀璨的星辰，那么隆恩殿就是这众星所拱护的月亮。隆恩殿居于方城的中心，前有隆恩门，后有大明楼，左右有东西配殿，四隅有角楼，显得异常雄伟。雕梁画栋，雄伟之余也增加了几许华贵。昭陵隆恩殿殿脊都装饰有一个仙人和一批走兽组成的吻兽，它们姿态各异，栩栩如生，活灵活现。一般吻兽领头是一位"仙人"，后面依次应为：龙、凤、狮子、天马、海马、狻猊、押鱼、獬豸、斗牛和行什。吻兽的安放有严格的等级制度，只有北京故宫的太和殿才能十样俱全，其他殿堂和寺庙建筑则要相应减少。昭陵隆恩殿殿脊有五个吻兽，而东西配殿则有三个，也有严格的等级区分。

当然，不仅仅是在建筑风格上，古时隆恩殿的主人也是整个昭陵甚至是当时中国最尊贵的人——墓主人太宗皇太极及孝端文皇后。作为清太祖努尔哈赤的第八个儿子，皇太极一生倥偬，于刀光马背之上挥斥方遒，在筹谋布阵之时施展抱负，终于创立了大清王朝。

努尔哈赤在统一女真，开疆拓土方面，是当之无愧的大英雄，但他是一位只识弯弓射大雕的君主；而皇太极不但重武功，更重文治，善于运筹帷幄。在领导风格方面，努尔哈赤实行与外戚联合的方式，利用暴力侵害其他民族的利益，获得政权；而皇太极则更加怀柔，努力将各个民族融合起来，一致对外，因而更加的昭明。我认为，这就是为什么昭陵无论在整体面积，还是在内部细节上都略胜福陵一筹的原因所在：得民心者得天下。从这个意义上说，皇太极比他父亲更具有中华民族整体的团结感和统一感，也更受百姓的爱戴。

有趣的是，每当昭陵举行大祭时，在隆恩殿内的供案两边各站着一位身穿朝服，腰胯配刀，全副武装的"侍卫"。这两人一位被称是"白大侠"，一位被称为"小侠"。别看大侠、小侠平日无别的职事，唯一的职责是在大祭时充当"御前侍卫"，可是，他们的爵位品级却很高。白大侠的官职是"世袭头等侍卫兼轻车都尉"，品级为正三品，与昭陵最高长官总管大人并列；小侠是"世袭头等侍卫兼骑都

昭陵隆恩殿／左图、上图
Eminent Favor Hall of Zhaoling Imperial Tomb / Left, Upper
清西陵（慕陵）隆恩殿／下图
Eminent Favor Hall of West Qing Mausoleum (Mu Mausoleum) / Lower

尉"，品级是从三品，比昭陵关防官大人还大半品。大侠、小侠都是世袭罔替，辈辈相传，第一位获得大侠封号的是"阿尔萨兰"，小侠名叫"商熙"，他们都是太宗皇太极生前的御前侍卫，忠臣的后代。关于忠臣，不能不提敦达里和安达里，皇太极死后，大臣敦达里"自愿"殉葬太宗皇太极，被列为"忠臣"典范，受到特殊礼遇，子孙因此世受殊荣。安达里本出身微贱，因战功屡受晋升。皇太极对他有"知遇"之恩，皇太极驾崩后，安达里效法敦达里，主动要求殉葬。今天在昭陵以西约1.5公里处，有两人的殉葬遗址。

隆恩殿里流传了很多故事，也遗失了很多故事，就像原来在隆恩殿须弥座的四角，对应上面的嘲风下各有一口大缸用来接水的。嘲风是龙之九子之老三，关于龙之九子，我在写《中国广告史》时研究论证过。现在昭陵隆恩殿四角，嘲风下面只有当初放置缸体的用石基雕成的缸座，缸座还在而缸已经

隆恩殿神道丹陛石／左图
Stair Stone on Spirit Path of Eminent Favor Hall / Left
隆恩殿旧照／右图
Old Picture of Eminent Favor Hall / Right

不知去向，不知道什么时候被什么人拿去做什么用了。现在雨雪天，积水会直接冲刷四角基石，"水滴石穿"，这对古建筑的保护是非常不利的。我想即使找不到当初的缸，也该放一个盛水的器皿在这个位置。最近一次去拍摄的时候，因为刚下过雨，地上圆形的缸座里盛满了水，远远看去像一个装水的盆子，使人一目了然此处的缺憾。

隆恩殿神道丹陛石／左页图
Stair Stone on Spirit Path of Eminent Favor Hall / Left Page
隆恩殿前石狮／上图
Stone Lion Statue in front of Eminent Favor Hall / Upper

HALL OF EMINENT FAVOR: RESTING PLACE FOR TAI TSU (EMPEROR HONG TAIJI) AND HIS EMPRESS

If the Mausoleum buildings of different styles are compared as shining stars of the sky, then Eminent Favor Hall can be deemed as the moon surrounded by these stars. Eminent Favor Hall is seated in the center of Square City with Eminent Favor Gate in front and Grand Ming Tower behind, East Side-hall and West Side-hall at both sides, and four Turrets in the four corners. All these buildings make Eminent Favor Hall extraordinarily spectacular while its carved beams and painted rafters add some nobleness. Ridges of the Hall are decorated with a celestial being and a group of wenshous (statues of dragons and other animals, found on the roofs of Chinese temples, palaces, and homes) with varied yet vivid postures. Wenshous usually follow a celestial being in order of dragon, phoenix, lion, heavenly steed, auspicious sea horse, suan ni (mythical lion), wind-and-storm-summoning fish, xie zhi, evil-dispelling bull and hang shi (mythical monkey with wings). Arrangement and decoration of wenshous should follow strict hierarchical rules and only Taihe Hall (Supreme Harmony Hall) of Forbidden City has all of them on roofs. Other buildings such as palaces and temples should reduce number of wenshous accordingly. There are only five wenshous on ridges of Eminent Favor Hall in Zhaoling Imperial Tomb while East Side-hall and West Side-hall have only three.

The prominence in architectural style of Eminent Favor Hall is self-evident, also thanks to its owner, Emperor Hong Taiji and Empress Xiaoduanwen, who were the most distinguished in that time of China.

隆恩殿须弥座嘲风／左页图
Chaofeng on Sumeru Base of Eminent Favor Hall / Upper Left Page
隆恩殿须弥座嘲风下缸座／左上图
Urn Base (for holding water) under Chaofeng of Eminent Favor Hall / Upper Left
安达里殉葬碑（沈阳故宫博物院藏）／右上图
Sacrificial Tombstone of An Dali (preserved in Shenyang Imperial Palace Museum) / Upper Right
嘲风后侧排水口／左下图
Drainage Hole behind Chaofeng / Lower Left
隆恩殿须弥座西南角嘲风／右下图
Chaofeng in the Southwestern Corner of Eminent Favor Hall / Lower Right

As the eighth son of Nurhaci, the forefather of Qing Dynasty, Emperor Hong Taiji had been fighting all his life on horsebacks and among hustling swords. Finally he fulfilled his ambition and established Qing Dynasty by fully tapping his talents and abilities.

In the process of unifying Jurchen ethnic group and expanding his territory, Nurhaci deserves the title of a great hero. However he is just a monarch proficient in fighting while his son Hong Taiji emphasizes both martial arts and cultural cultivation and can always play his cards right. In ruling the country, Nurhaci focuses on unifying distant relatives and suppressing other nationalities. On the contrary, Hong Taiji highlights conciliation and unification of different races. He tries to unify all ethnic groups to fight against enemies, displaying keen intelligence and excellent judgment. That justifies why Zhaoling Imperial Tomb is superior to Fu Mausoleum in both size and inner decoration and proves "whoever gain the common aspiration of the people can rule the country." In this sense, Emperor Hong Taiji's ruling makes Chinese nation more unified and further consolidated, and he is therefore worshipped by common people.

What is funny is that whenever the Mausoleum hosted a grand sacrifice, there would be a fully armed "imperial bodyguard" standing on either side of the altar inside Eminent Favor Hall: one was called "White Swordsman," the other "Little Swordsman." Their only job was to stand as "imperial bodyguard" on the occasion of sacrifice. However, their rank of nobility was high with White Swordsman's title as "Hereditary First-class Imperial Bodyguard & Light Chariots Caid" (Principal Third Rank), equivalent with the chief official of Zhaoling Imperial Tomb. And the Little Swordsman's title was "Hereditary First-class Imperial Bodyguard & Riding Caid" (Subsidiary Third Rank), a half class higher than a Zhaoling Imperial Tomb Border Official. Both titles were hereditary. The first man with the title of White Swordsman was Arsalan and the one with the title of Little Marshal was Shangxi, both of whom were descendants of loyal officials and imperial bodyguards of Hong Taiji. Speaking of loyal officials, Dun Dali and An Dali are worth mentioning. Duan, of his own will, sacrificed for Hong Taiji's death and thus he was ranked as "loyal official" and his offsprings were treated with special honor. An, from a humble origin, was promoted several times for his brilliant achievements in war. He followed suit to show his gratitude to Hong Taiji. Relics of their sacrifice can be found about 1.5 km east of Zhaoling Imperial Tomb.

There are a lot of legendary stories regarding Eminent Favor Hall, such as its four corners of the Hall's Sumeru throne. Under each Chaofeng of the Sumeru throne, a large urn used to be placed underneath to hold falling water. According to Chinese legends, Chaofeng is a reckless and adventurous dragon whose image can be seen decorating the eaves of palaces. It is said to be the third son of Dragon King who has nine sons, which has been referred to in my book *A History of Chinese Advertising*. Currently, the urn has gone, but its base retains. In snowy and rainy days, the water will scour the footstone of the Hall. "Dripping water penetrates the stone," so it is harmful to the heritage building. In my opinion, even original urns are lost; pots and the like should be placed there to hold water. The last time when I came to take photos, it was raining. The urn base, looked from afar, seemed like a water basin, making the defect of urn loss most obvious.

隆恩殿须弥座嘲风／左图
Chaofeng on Sumeru Base of Eminent Favor Hall / Left
昭西陵隆恩殿须弥座嘲风没有吐水功能／右上图
Chaofeng (without Function of Drainage) on Sumeru Base of Eminent Favor Hall of West Zhao Mausoleum / Upper Right
隆恩殿须弥座栏杆上的盘龙旧照／右下图
Old Picture of Intertwined Dragons on Sumeru-based Rails of Eminent Favor Hall / Lower Right

皇孙膝下的拜石

皇家陵园的豪气与壮观在昭陵的各个建筑中都能够得以体现，但是若说到尊贵非凡，却不得不提到隆恩殿中的拜石。古往今来，很多来此体验清朝文化的游客都曾经从这块拜石边走过，甚至抚摸着它，感受那种沉淀于历史中的细腻，但是又有多少人知道，这块拜石竟是用价值连城的纯翡翠制成的呢？真是男儿膝下有黄金，皇孙膝下有翡翠。

"翡翠玉拜石，当年国富修"，清同治年间刊印的《陪都纪略》（注解11）就曾经这样评价过此拜石。色彩斑斓，通透耀眼的拜石是当时从缅甸国进贡来的，名贵而罕见，甚至引起了欧美一些外国考察团的关注，他们称赞这块石头为"难得之品，天成之物"。不仅如此，其体积之大，保存之完整，也是世间罕见的，透过这块翡翠拜石，我仿佛可以穿越时空，看到当时清朝的太平盛世，天下来拜的霸气与威严。缅甸距离当时的都城沈阳非常远，而这块拜石又如此巨大，究竟如何将它运送来的呢？这也是一个困扰我的难题，不过或许正是这种"不可思议"才能证明清朝的强大与繁荣，才能彰显出泱泱大国的不凡威慑。

这小小的一块拜石，在清代却似乎备受皇家重视。对于拜石，昭陵、福陵和永陵是置之于殿外，孝陵的拜石则是一半在殿内，一半在殿外，其他清帝的陵墓基本都将其置于隆恩殿内，然而无论其身处何处，都能够体现出它独特的尊贵地位。

清西陵（慕陵）隆恩殿拜石 / 左图
Worship Stone inside Eminent Favor Hall of East Qing Mausoleum (Mu Mausoleum) / Left
昭西陵拜石在室内 三块 / 右图
Three Worship Stones inside West Zhao Mausoleum / Right
隆恩殿须弥座上的翡翠拜石 / 右页图
Worship Stone of Jade on Sumeru Base inside Eminent Favor Hall / Right Page

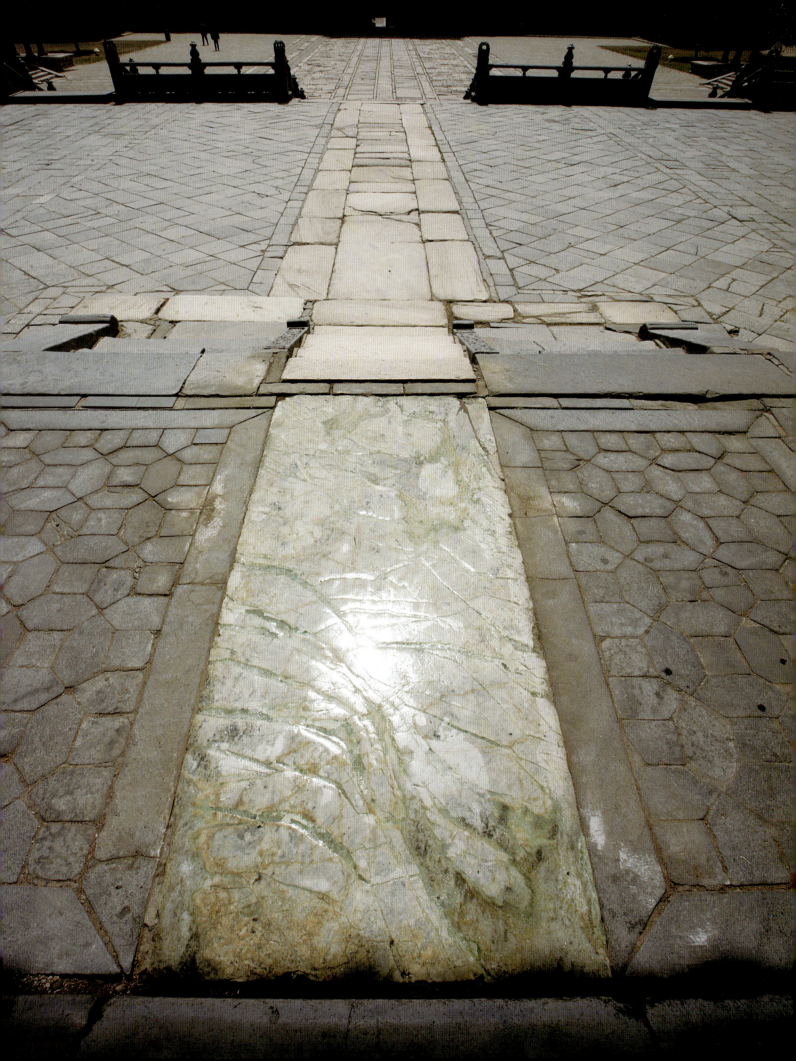

隆恩殿内／左页图
Inside Eminent Favor Hall / Left Page
隆恩殿旧照／左图
Old Picture of Eminent Favor Hall / Left
隆恩殿内乾隆进献的神灯／右图
Lamp Offered by Emperor Qianlong inside Eminent Favor Hall / Right

WORSHIP STONE UNDER KNEES OF IMPERIAL DESCENDANTS

Majesty and splendor of the imperial mausoleums can be embodied through every building inside. Worship Stone inside Eminent Favor Hall is worth mentioning for its extraordinary dignity. Throughout the ages, many visitors passed by the Stone, fondled it, and sensed its delicacy accumulated through history, but few know that the Stone is made out of a priceless pure jade. It can be said that there is gold under a man's knees and jade under those of imperial descendants.

"Worship stone of jade, symbol of power in those days." The Stone has been appraised in the book Memoirs of Shengjing (see Note 11) printed during the reign of Emperor Tongzhi in Qing Dynasty. Gorgeous crystal-like Worship Stone was a tribute from Burma. The Stone is so precious and rare that it aroused attention from European and U.S. delegates who praised it as "rare gem, making of nature." Its size and completeness are also rare in the world. Through the jade, I seem to see through history and catch sight of the prosperous Qing Dynasty as well as its supremeness and dignity. Burma is far away from the capital city Shenyang of the time and how did the people manage to transport such a huge jade stone here? However, it is the very "inconceivableness" that reveals the prosperity and powerfulness of Qing Dynasty and exhibits her unusual magnificence as a great country.

This little Worship Stone had been much valued by the royal family of Qing Dynasty. Worship Stones in Zhaoling Imperial Tomb, Fu Mausoleum and Yong Mausoleum are all located outside Eminent Favor Hall while that in Xiao Mausoleum is located with its half inside Eminent Favor Hall and the other half outside the Hall. Worship Stones in other mausoleums are all located inside Eminent Favor Hall. However, regardless of where they are located, their unique noble status are well demonstrated.

皇太极与博尔济吉特氏的世代姻缘

在婚姻问题上，皇太极与父亲努尔哈赤的做法也大有差别。努尔哈赤甚至杀死了自己妻子的哥哥、皇太极的舅舅布扬古，而皇太极却以和谐的方式处理夫妻关系。这隆恩殿里的女主人就是皇太极的正妻——孝端文皇后博尔济吉特氏。皇太极，起初写作"黄台吉"，皇太极这个名字是他继承汗位以后才传开的。"台吉"一词源于蒙古语，意思相当于汉语中的"太师"，蒙古人把可汗的继承人称为"台吉"。蒙古人愿意在名字前加颜色，而汉族人把皇帝尊为最高统治者，皇太极这个名字，是和当时的满蒙汉文化融合分不开的，比起努尔哈赤的名字"野猪皮"要更有政治意义和文化意义。其实从努尔哈赤开始，就开始了与蒙古部分王公世代通婚的历史，利用政治联姻来巩固自己的疆域所有权，而皇太极的这位皇后，正是蒙古科尔沁的贝勒莽古思之女。虽然她一生既没有突出的功绩，也没有被卷入宫闱是非之中，甚至可以说是完全被淹没在皇家争妍斗艳、钩心斗角的后宫历史之中，然而就是这种宁静淡泊的心态，成就了她与众不同的大度与庄重，因而深得皇太极的赞赏。

遗憾的是，皇后与皇太极成婚12年却终无所出，于是她决定将自己的两个亲侄女布木布泰和海兰珠嫁给自己的丈夫，此后便有了一段段让世人感慨至今的皇家故事。她当时怎么也不会想到，小侄女布木布泰成为后来垂帘听政的庄妃，大侄女海兰珠则成为皇太极心口一颗永远的朱砂痣。

关于皇太极的婚姻，在很多人眼中，姑侄三人共侍一夫，有人在故宫解说词中说这是一种乱伦。这个观点我不赞同，我们不能用民间的婚俗观点看待帝王的婚姻。

帝王贵为一国之君，伴随君主这个称呼而来的，除了只手遮天的权力，还有牺牲诸多自由的无奈。君主的婚姻古往今来，都是一种稳固政治、融合异族的手段，情爱次之。清朝政权建立之初，政权极不稳定，皇太极先后娶了七位蒙古族的嫔妃，这其中就有与蒙古族建立政治联盟的含义。而且，我们也不能用我们时下的婚姻制度去衡量兄弟民族的婚姻。无论是皇太极所在的女真族，或是嫔妃们所属的蒙古族，在当时都有"转房婚"这一习俗，在当时是北方民族普遍存在的一种习俗，较普遍的有妻兄弟婚，夫姊妹婚等。这种现象在现代也有着不同形式的演绎，著名表演艺术家赵丽蓉老师的两任丈夫就是一对亲兄弟。其实要是真说起来，唐明皇迎娶了儿媳妇杨玉环，甚至比皇太极娶姑侄三人更加让人不能理解，但是后人不但没有指责他们的爱情，甚至赋《长恨歌》来颂之，为什么到了皇太极这里就是乱伦呢？登基后皇太极因受汉族文化影响，废弃了原来的婚俗观念，说"既生为人，若娶族中妇女；与禽兽何异"，他下令："自今（1636年）以后，凡人不许娶庶母及族中伯母、婶母、嫂子、媳妇"，"凡女人若丧夫，欲守其家资、子女者，由本人（家）宜思养；若欲改嫁者，本家无人看管，任族中兄弟聘于异性之人。若不遵法，族中相娶者，与奸淫一例问罪"。这样才形成了民族融合为特色的新的婚姻习俗，并成为满族婚姻制度及其礼俗的主流，一直持续到近代。但是在黑龙江，部分满族仍袭旧俗，女子若嫁上一辈人，被认为是抬辈，是一件荣耀的事。一般舅舅家的女儿可以嫁给姑母家的儿子，姑母做婆，姑母家的女儿却不准嫁给舅舅家的儿子，认为这是骨血倒流。

皇太极一生都致力于民族融合，不同于他的父亲——努尔哈赤一生防守疆土，不允许外族的进入，和外戚是一种坚决对峙的态度，但皇太极通过自己娶亲的方式，贯彻着民族融合的政策，更具雄韬伟略。融合了众多民族后，他创立了一个新的民族——满族。

其实，对于现在的中国来说，汉族、满族、蒙古族、朝鲜族、回族等都是兄弟民族，正如歌曲中歌颂的那样：兄弟民族是一家。

昭西陵正红门遗址
Relics of Front Red Gate in West Zhao Mausoleum

太宗文皇帝皇太极像 / 左图
Paintings of Emperor Taizong, Hong Taiji / Left
庄妃像 / 右图
Painting of Concubine Zhuang / Right

MARRIAGES OF HONG TAIJI WITH BORJIGIT HALA

Hong Taiji and his father Nurhaci were quite different in dealing with marital problems. Nurhaci had even killed Buyanggu, his wife's brother, Hong Taiji's maternal uncle, while Hong Taiji could deal with spousal relationship in a harmonious way. Hostess of Eminent Favor Hall is the legal wife of Hong Taiji – Empress Xiaoduanwen, Borjigit Hala. Hong Taiji (皇太极) was formerly called as Huang Taiji (黄台吉). Hong Taiji, as a name, was not widely used until he succeeded to Khan. Taiji originated from Mongolian, a title addressed to those who were supposed to succeed to Khan. And the Mongolian people liked to put a color word in front (Huang means yellow) and thus came the name. The Chinese character 皇 is used by Han nationality to refer to an emperor. So the name of Hong Taiji was actually the result of cultural hybrid. Compared with the name of Nurhaci (which means fur of wild boar in Manchu), Hong Taiji as a name bears more political and cultural implications. In fact, Nurhaci started internuptial history with Mongolian nobility during his ruling period, consolidating his rule through intermarriage while Hong Taiji's wife was the daughter of Manggus – Mongolian baylor (a rank of Manchu nobility below that of Prince) of Khorchin. Borjigit Hala had neither prominent feats nor conflicting dispute of palace chambers, and she was even neglected in the struggling history of maneuver for positions against rival concubines. It was right her serenity and simplicity that makes her a different woman with magnanimousness and solemnity, and thus wins the heartfelt favor of Hong Taiji.

Pitifully, Empress and Hong Taiji had no offspring during their 12 years of marriage. So she decided to marry her nieces Bumbutai and Hailanzhu to her husband. She might have never expected that Bumbutai attended to state affairs later and Hailanzhu became a forever cinnabar mole in the heart of Hong Taiji.

In the eyes of many people, the marriages were disgraceful considering the fact that the aunt and her nieces married Hong Taiji as his wives. Some people even claim it fornication in their captions of the imperial palace. But personally I am not in favor of the viewpoint, as we cannot view the marriage of emper-

神龛、宝座／左页图
Niche and Throne / Left Page
隆恩殿内玉制香炉（复制品）／左上图
隆恩殿内银制香炉（复制品）／中上图
隆恩殿内铜制香炉（复制品）／右上图
Duplicates of Incense Burners (Jade, Silver, Bronze) / Upper Left, Upper Middle & Upper Right
清东陵孝陵祭祀表演／下图
Sacrificial Rites Performance Held in Xiao Mausoleum (East Qing Mausoleum) / Lower

ors from the perspective of a civilian's eyes.

What comes with the royal crown is not only the supreme right, but also the helplessness and sacrifice of freedom. Marriages of ancient emperors were, as often as not, used as means to stabilize politics and unify difference races, i.e. love of emperor usually gave way to politics. At the founding time of Qing Dynasty, Emperor Hong Taiji married seven Mongolian concubines with a view of allying with Mongolians, as the regime was not stable at that time. Hong Taiji belonged to Jurchen ethnic group, and his concubines belonged to the Mongolians. Both ethnicities then practiced the custom of levirate marriage. It has different renderings in contemporary society, for example, famous actress Zhao Lirong's husband and ex-husband are brothers. To be more specific, Emperor Ming of Tang Dynasty married his daughter-in-law, which was not only under criticism but also eulogized by the great poet Bai Juyi in Everlasting Regret. How was Hong Taiji claimed to be immoral? That is because Han culture deems it immoral to marry a woman of one's own clan. Later, influenced by Han customs, Hong Taiji deserted his previous marital conventions and enacted, "From now on (1636), it is forbidden to marry a paternal uncle's wife and daughter-in-law, or sister-in-law," "If a woman lost her husband and she wants to defend the family property and kids, she will be supported by the family; if she remarries, her family members will hire people of another clan to take care of the family," "Those who break the rules and marry family people will be punished for adultery." Thus a new marriage custom was formed and became the main stream of Manchu's marriage system, which is followed till now. However, in Heilongjiang Province, some Manchu still practice their traditional customs. If a girl marries to her senior generation, it will be regarded as an honor for her as it promotes her status. Generally, maternal uncle's daughters can get married with a paternal aunt's son, and the paternal aunt will serve as mother-in-law. A paternal aunt's daughter cannot get married with a maternal uncle's son, as it is deemed a reverse flow of blood.

Hong Taiji dedicated all his life to ethnic fusion

隆恩殿内神龛、神位 / 左页图
Niche and Memorial Tablet inside Eminent Favor Hall / Left Page
隆恩殿内神龛、神位、神座旧照 / 上图
Old Pictures of Niche and Memorial Tablet inside Eminent Favor Hall / Upper

while his father Nurhaci was a hardliner, who had defended his territory in his lifetime, preventing invasion of aliens and holding a hard attitude against consort clan. Hong Taiji adopted and carried out the policy of national unification by means of intermarriage, which exhibited his great strategy. After unifying many ethnic groups, he established a new one – Manchu.

In fact, for present-day China, Ethnic Groups such as Han, Manchu, Mongolian, Korean, and Hui are all brother ethnicities, just as a line in a song: Brother ethnicities are of one family.

隆恩殿内沥粉贴金彩绘／左图、上图
Embossed and Gilded Colored Painting of Eminent Favor Hall / Left, Upper

清西陵（慕陵）隆恩殿／下图
Eminent Favor Hall of West Qing Mausoleum (Mu Mausoleum) / Lower

皇太极最爱的牌位都无权进入东配殿

东配殿在隆恩殿东厢，在陵寝中的地位仅次于隆恩殿。我小时一直认为昭陵里的正殿是为皇太极和皇后所建，那么，东西配殿的主人理所应当与故宫里的建筑布局一样，即东配殿是海兰珠，西配殿是庄妃。

2003年8月申遗前，昭陵最西侧的一处遗址被挖掘，说是贵妃园，当时我正住院术后修养，我决定出院跟着考古队一起考察。那一刻，我的心情很复杂。

昭陵贵妃园，原名叫宸妃、懿靖大贵妃园寝，位于宝城以西约百米处，相比之下，福陵也有一个康寿妃园寝，在今天的后陵前堡村，离陵寝相对更远些。昭陵贵妃园内有土丘十一座，埋葬着皇太极的嫔妃，而其中的三位在清初历史上很有名望，她们分别是关雎宫的宸妃，麟趾宫的贵妃和衍庆宫的淑妃。懿靖大贵妃，博尔济吉特氏，名娜木钟，蒙古阿巴亥郡王额齐格诺颜之女，她和淑妃一样初嫁察哈尔林丹汗，史称"囊囊太后"，林丹汗在天聪六年死于青海大草原后，娜木钟归降皇太极，并被纳为妃子。崇德元年，被封麟趾宫贵妃，福临继位后晋封为"太妃"，福临亲政，加封太妃尊号为"懿靖大贵妃"。康熙十三年崩，梓宫送盛京火化，归葬昭陵贵妃园寝。当年日本学者考证，园寝南北长49.78米，东西宽27.6米。根据《奉天昭陵图谱》一书，贵妃园寝呈长方形，坐北朝南，四面红墙围绕。南北有红门，院内有享殿，享殿东西两侧是果房和茶膳房，都是祭祀时存放祭品的用房。遗憾的是，如今的贵妃园仅存遗址，几乎被埋没在荒草中，拍摄柱础时，看见上面已长着巨大的树根，看不出当年皇家陵寝的痕迹了。

如果说历代皇朝组成了一幅风诡云谲、波澜迭起的宏伟画卷，那么后宫的万千红颜则勾勒出了这幅画卷上最为美丽细腻的花边。而皇太极的两个女人，宸妃和庄妃这对姊妹花，则各自绽放着属于自己的独特光彩，直到今天仍被人津津乐道。海兰珠，虽然入宫时间比妹妹晚，但是她仍然凭借自己的娇弱柔美获得皇太极的宠爱。然而都说天妒红颜，在儿子夭折后的第三年，海兰珠也郁郁而终在后宫的繁华虚浮中，因为挚爱的儿子的离去而丧失活下去的勇气，是多么让人心疼的一种纯洁和倔强，海兰珠的死，将一份深入骨髓的疼痛留给了皇太极一个人品尝。连向来忌讳涉及后宫之事的史书都说："太宗方伐明，闻宸妃病而还，未至，妃已薨，上恸甚"，能够让这个戎马一生的男人弃战而归，心碎流泪，英雄美人的爱情故事演绎到这份上，真的足够让人动容。

难道海兰珠等妃子的牌位都在贵妃园么？会不会如故宫一样，放在东配殿呢？后来我研究才知道东配殿的实际用途，是用来存放祝版和制帛，隆恩殿大修时，也存放神牌。东配殿作为配殿，但在特殊的情况下可以代替隆恩殿。当隆恩殿进行大修时，要将殿内供奉的太宗及皇后两座神牌由隆恩殿迁至东配殿暂时供奉。直到完工以后，还要举行仪式将神牌重新请回隆恩殿。即使平时空着，其他妃子的牌位也是不能放在这里的。

东配殿神龛／上图
Niche inside East Side-hall / Upper

东配殿／右图
East Side-hall / Right

EAST SIDE-HALL, NOT FOR MEMORIAL TABLETS OF HONG TAIJI'S FAVORITE CONCUBINES

East Side-hall is located at the east wing and only second to Eminent Favor Hall in position. I had held the belief in my childhood that the main hall, i.e. Eminent Favor Hall, was built for Emperor Hong Taiji and his Empress, and then its East Side-hall and West Side-hall should be for Concubine Chen (Hanlanzhu) and Concubine Zhuang respectively, the same architectural composition as Forbidden City.

Before the application of Zhaoling Imperial Tomb as World Cultural Heritage in August of 2003, a site at the utmost east side of the Mausoleum was excavated, which was said to be Noble Concubines Garden. Although I was then in rehabilitation after a surgery, I decided to observe and study the site along with the archaeological team.

Noble Concubines Garden of Zhaoling Imperial Tomb were once called Garden of Concubine Chen and Imperial Consort Yijing, hundreds of meters away to the west of Blessed City. In contrast, Fu Mausoleum also has a Concubine Kangshou Garden at the present Qibao Village of Houling Town, and the distance of the Garden to the Mausoleum is a little farther. There are altogether 11 mounds inside Noble Concubines Garden with Hong Taiji's concubines buried inside, three of whom are well known in history: Concubine Chen of Guanju Palace, Imperial Consort of Linzhi Palace and Concubine Shu of Yanqing Palace. Imperial Consort Yijing from tribe of Borjigit, named Namuzhong, was a daughter of Ecige Nuoyan, Chief of Abbahai County, Mongolia. Like Concubine Shu, she married Chahar Lindan Khan, known as "Queen Mother Nangnang" in history. Lindan Khan died in Qinghai plateau at the sixth year of Emperor Tiancong. Namuzhong was remarried with Hong Taiji as a concubine. On the first year of Emperor Chongde, she was granted as Imperial Consort of Linzhi Palace. After Prince Fulin enthroned, she was honored as "Great Concubine," and later entitled with "Imperial Consort Yijing." She died on the 13th ruling year of Emperor Kangxi; her coffin was sent to Mukden for cremation and then buried in Noble Concubines Garden of Zhaoling Imperial Tomb. According to the records of a Japanese scholar, the garden is 49.78 meters long and 27.6 meters wide. According to Atlas of Mukden Zhaoling Imperial Tomb, the mausoleum in Noble Concubines Garden was rectangular, facing south, surrounded by red walls. Red gates were set in the north and south and Enjoyment Hall was built inside. At the east and west sides of the Palace were Fruit House and Tea House, serving the purpose of storing oblations during sacrifices. The Garden has been in ruins now, covered up by wilderness with its grandeur of imperial tomb lost a long time ago.

If the successive dynasties in history are compared as a magnificent scroll with eerie clouds and surging waves, then those countless beauties of the imperial harem have embroidered the most beautiful and delicate laces for it. The two favorite concubines of Hong Taiji, Zhuang and Chen, distinguished themselves in their own way, which are still the delight of people's talking even today. Hailanzhu entered the imperial palace later than her sister, but with her gentle and feminine beauty, she won the favor of Hong Taiji. An old saying in China goes like this, "God is jealous of those who are pretty." On the third year after her beloved son's death, Hailanzhu lost her confidence in life, and withered away amidst the bustling yet flatulent imperial harem. Her heartbreaking death left Hong Taiji with innermost unbearable pain. According to historical records, which rarely wrote about lives of imperial harem, "The Emperor was at the point of conquering Ming Dynasty, but on hearing of Chen's heavy illness, he galloped back hastily. Before he could arrive at her sickbed, she passed away. The emperor was dumb-stricken and heartbroken." It is a striking story about a hero and his beauty, whose death called back Hong Taiji who had spent all his life on horseback fighting for the state power. The story of tearful and heartbroken Hong illustrates how Concubine Chen was cherished in Hong Taiji's heart.

Is it possible that memorial tablets of Hailanzhu and other concubines of Hong Taiji were placed in Noble Concubines Garden? Or were they worshipped in East Side-hall as the case of Forbidden City? These questions were solved after I had studied the actual functions of East Side-hall. The hall was actually used to keep Prayer Tablets and other sacrificial silks, or memorial tablets of emperor and empress when Eminent Favor Hall was under repair. As a wing hall, East Side-hall could play the role of Eminent Favor Hall. When Eminent Favor Hall was renovated, memorial tablets of emperor and empress would be moved to East Side-hall until completion of the repair. Memorial tablets of other concubines would never be set here even if it was not occupied.

皇帝生母的牌位也无权进入西配殿

西配殿在隆恩殿西厢，共五间，建筑样式与东配殿相同。当我知道东配殿供的不是海兰珠时，我以为是因为她没有子嗣；而西配殿里可能供着庄妃的牌位，因为她是顺治帝的生母，康熙帝的祖母。

庄妃，博尔济吉特氏布木布泰，她的前半生并不出彩，丈夫生前已经把所有的爱都给了她的姐姐海兰珠，死后能够留给她的，只有一个尚未更事的皇太子——福临。面对巨大的权势诱惑，她没有像武则天那样打破世俗成规，自己登基称帝，庄妃选择的是一条更加辛苦而无私的道路，默默地辅佐儿子，尽心竭力，万苦不辞。也许是因为这么伟大的一个女人在感情方面却一片空白，人们便不甘心让她的传说就这样落寞下去，于是给她附会了一段凄美的爱情故事：和睿亲王多尔衮的情感纠葛，但事实究竟如何，恐怕只有她自己最清楚。庄妃是一个女人，然而在那个男尊女卑的年代，她也是一个政治人物，因为她在史书上刚一出现，就已经承载着政治，承载了清皇朝的权力纷争，被历史的洪潮推着，她只能让自己更加坚强，为儿子和孙子撑起一片天空。而那些撰写历史的男人通常会把过错扣在无辜的女人头上，殷纣王昏庸无道，唐玄宗好色误国，屠刀却砍在妲己和玉环的头上，历史惯用女人的鲜血洗涤男人的罪恶。同是扶助小皇帝，男人则是辅佐朝政，功盖天下；女人则是把持朝政，作乱纲常。褪去历史的浮云，庄妃有胆有识，一生中成功地辅佐了三代帝王，为康乾盛世打造了稳固的根基，可以说，她是一位传奇式的蒙古族杰出女性。

康熙二十六年（1687 年），博尔济吉特家族的伟大女人庄妃去世，然而令人不解的是，她死后并没有葬于昭陵之中，嘱托孙子康熙无须将她与皇太极合葬，因此直到康熙帝死，也未给祖母孝庄文皇后建陵，最终于雍正三年（1725 年）才由曾孙胤禛安葬于清东陵的风水墙外的地宫内。庄妃未葬于昭陵，也一直为学者所困惑，成为历史难解之谜。

我仔细思索着，庄妃，一个伟大女人的一生，为何在临终前要对孙子做出令人费解的嘱托，不愿与丈夫合葬。困惑许久之后的一天，在我的思绪停留在贵妃园的时候，我突然豁然开朗，激动之情，喜形于色。我想，大概是这样吧。应该说庄妃在皇太极时代并不得宠，之所以有后来的功绩，都归功于她的儿子。若没有生下日后做了皇帝的儿子，恐怕她再有政治抱负，也将会和所有后宫佳丽的命运一样，埋没于万丈宫墙内，埋没于历史尘烟中，除了史书上的一笔名字，甚至连踪迹都无可查循。但是，命运还是垂青了她，没有轰轰烈烈的爱情，却给了她改变命运的皇子。于是，她可以一展抱负，辅佐三代君王，打下康乾盛世基础，被人们尊为伟大的女人。她的后半生，都处在至高无上的位置，无论是权势还是名望都堪比当年的武则天，她怎能不思索身后事？按清代等级森严的皇家制度，皇帝以下的陵都叫园寝，即只有皇帝的墓才可称为陵，而只有皇后才有资格与皇帝同葬陵内，而庄妃不过是皇太极并不怎么宠爱的妃子，当年的皇后是她的亲姑姑，这一点，聪明如她，怎会想不到？按受宠而言，她不及她的姐姐，甚至比不了后来的林丹汗的两位妃子，如此一来，她将葬于何处？此时处于至尊地位的庄妃，又怎么能忍受死后被埋没于地位不及她的众妃子园中？于是，她便想到了就近安葬自己的主意，以"太宗在盛京已经安葬很久了，不要再为我打开地宫与之合葬了，我因为惦念你们父子（指顺治和康熙），不愿远离"的理由嘱咐孙子康熙。康熙帝如此孝顺孝庄，却没能在有生之年为祖母找到一块万年吉地，难道真的是他贵为一国之君而没有能力吗？恐怕不是康熙皇帝的能力问题，而是在祖制与祖母的遗愿之间两难吧，按清朝祖制孝庄死后应归葬昭陵。也有人说庄妃是因为下嫁给多尔衮才不能归葬昭陵的，而下嫁一说已经被证明是虚构的野史。还有人说，庄妃是害怕火葬，才要求不回昭陵。我认为害怕火葬一说更是没有道理，庄妃曾亲历自己的丈夫与儿子的火葬，不能拿百姓之心度君王之意。历史上最有权势的女人，武则天作为皇帝也没有为自己单独建陵。而孝庄却要求孙子给自己单独建一座陵，可见在历史的舞台上，她才是那个隐藏最深的真正的狠角色。在关内，也因此有了昭西陵，这座与自己丈夫陵寝相距万里之遥又区别于清东陵和清西陵的独特陵寝。听说在昭陵贵妃园中，还有一座空坟，不知是不是当年为庄妃准备的。可以说是庄妃开创了大清朝的一个新的制度，而在庄妃之前，清朝还没有单独给皇后建陵的。

提到皇后陵，就不能不提孝东陵。孝东陵是顺治帝的后妃墓地，里边葬着孝惠章皇后和28位妃子、格格、福晋。孝东陵建成后，初称"新陵"，并不是由朝廷正式命名的。孝惠章皇后葬入地宫后，改称"孝惠章皇后陵"，直到康熙五十八年（1719年），礼部向皇帝奏本说："古来帝后有不合葬而自为陵者，俱就方位定名。今孝惠章皇后陵既在孝陵之东，不必另立陵名。臣等恭拟'孝东陵'字样，仰候钦定。"康熙帝同意了这个奏本，从此孝惠章皇后陵正式称孝东陵。孝东陵，实际上有着贵妃园的特点，葬有很多妃子，而昭西陵则是真正意义上的单独的皇后陵。史料中也有关于给庄妃建陵一事的记载，尤其是命名问题，证明当时清朝对给皇后建陵制度并不熟悉而只好仿造前朝。那就是皇后也可以单独建陵，只是仍然要以丈夫的陵名加以方位来定名。因皇太极陵寝为昭陵，故庄妃陵寝为昭西陵。西，是相对于沈阳方向说的。而北京的清东陵与清西陵则是相对于北京来说的，就如同沈阳的东陵与北陵一样。又如雍正帝皇后孝圣宪皇后的泰东陵位于雍正帝的泰陵东北约1.5公里处。还有一个特别的例子，就是恭亲王奕訢的母亲，因为咸丰帝给封了后，就在贵妃园寝中加了墙，单独成陵了。

站在历史角度看，无论是稳重的孝端文皇后，还是娇弱的海兰珠和坚强的庄妃布木布泰，她们都是伟大的女人，都是蒙古族的骄傲，庄妃也为后来的慈禧做了榜样。清朝的慈禧太后也曾经辅佐过三位皇帝：咸丰、同治和妹妹的儿子光绪。武则天一生机关算尽，为求权政不惜先杀女再杀子；而庄妃和慈禧则是垂帘听政，这与自己登基做皇帝有着本质上的差别。

昭陵西配殿，即使是皇帝生母，历史上最有权势的女人之一，庄妃的牌位，也是无权存放在这里的。而西配殿的真正用途，是作为喇嘛们诵经作法超度亡灵的地方。努尔哈赤生前信奉喇嘛教，皇太极时期为笼络蒙古更是不遗余力地推崇之。女真族最原始的信仰是萨满教，后来随着政治与联姻的需要，信仰有所改变，信喇嘛教，有利于团结蒙古、青海、西藏等地。北京的雍和宫，原来是雍王府，即雍正皇帝登基前的家，乾隆帝在此出生。雍和宫在乾隆九年改为喇嘛庙，成为全国最高级别的佛教寺庙。而乾隆因为香妃的缘故，还在圆明园修建了清真寺。清朝历代皇室之所以都极力推崇佛教，也是为了国家一统的目的。

后来我经过研究发现，陵寝里的建筑和故宫里台上五宫的建筑用途大相径庭。东西配殿在建筑布局上，依傍着正殿，在建筑形式上相互承继，互相补充。正因为东西配殿并不是我想的那样，存放妃子牌位的地方，我想这也是衣食无忧的皇室斗争为什么异常激烈的原因所在。除了皇后，其他嫔妃连进方城的资格都没有，都在红墙外，包括皇太极的最爱海兰珠都只能葬在贵妃园。平常百姓争的可能是感情和财产，而皇室中的争斗则是生死利益的争斗，是几个家族与利益集团之间的斗争，是青史留名的地位之争。

当年，我们还在贵妃园挖到过一个骨灰罐，这些宫妃贵人，生前争宠争利，后宫仿佛就是没有硝烟的战场，大家非要争个你死我活，国破家亡。死后，尸骨无存，或者只有这么一个罐子，而连名姓都无从考证，也不知是不是海兰珠的，还是哪位妃子的，想来也是件伤感的事。我们把她暂放在隆恩殿内，让她魂聚一回，尽管不合"礼制"，却也别无安放之处。

西配殿／左页图、左下图
West Side-hall / Left Page, Lower Left
昭西陵庄妃庙号碑／右下图
Stele of Temple Title for Concubine Zhuang in West Zhao Mausoleum / Lower Right

WEST SIDE-HALL, NOT EVEN FOR MEMORIAL TABLET OF EMPEROR'S MOTHER

West Side-hall is at the west wing, and it has five rooms with the same architectural style as East Side-hall. I had thought the reason that East Side-hall was not for memorial tablet of Hailanzhu was that she lost no imperial son, and West Side-hall should be for memorial tablet of Concubine Zhuang, for she was the mother of Emperor Shunzhi and grandmother of Emperor Kangxi.

Borjigit Hala Bumbutai, or Concubine Zhuang, lived her first half of life unremarkably. Her husband favored her elder sister Hailanzhu throughout his life. What he left her after his death was a toddling Prince Fulin. Concubine Zhuang ignored the inviting temptations of power and influence, acting totally different from Empress Wu Zetian of Tang Dynasty who sought the crown, and she assisted his son to rule the country arduously and silently, which was in fact an even tougher road. People fabricated love stories for her, quoting that she had a love affair with Dorgon. However, nobody knows it for sure. As a woman and a political figure at a time that women were deemed inferior to men, Concubine Zhuang braved the storms and clashes of throne when she was pushed to the front stage of history. She had no choice but to be stronger and support her son and grandson to stand up to all challenges. Men that recorded history often blamed women for the failure of a country, like Daji of Yin Dynasty and Yang Yuhuan of Tang Dynasty. The innocent women were often killed finally while the fatuous or amative emperors were spared. It was taken for granted that if a man assisted a young emperor to run a country, he would win acclaims; and if it came to a woman, it would violate feudal ethical codes. Ambitious and bold, Concubine Zhuang helped three generations of emperors, laying a solid foundation for grand prosperity of Emperor Kangxi and Emperor Qianlong. She was an outstanding legendary Mongolian heroine.

On the 26th ruling year of Emperor Kangxi (1687), the great woman Concubine Zhuang ceased to exist. What puzzles us most is why she was not buried in Zhaoling Imperial Tomb with Hong Taiji. She willed her grandson Emperor Kangxi not to place her body together with Hong Taiji. And therefore a mausoleum for her, grandmother of Emperor Kangxi, was not built, even after the death of Emperor Kangxi himself. It was not until the 3rd ruling year of Emperor Yongzheng (1725), that Concubine Zhuang was buried in the underground palace outside the geomantic wall of East Mausoleum. The fact that Concubine Zhuang was not buried in Zhaoling Imperial Tomb became an unsolvable riddle in history, confusing many scholars.

I tried to find the answer why this great woman was unwilling to be buried together with her husband. One day when I strolled around Noble Concubines Garden, I was suddenly enlightened. My reasoning goes like as follows. Concubine Zhuang had not been favored by Hong Taiji, and she attributed all her feats to her son. Without the birth of her son, she would make no difference with other concubines despite her ambition. She gave birth to the prince who absolutely changed her life. She was respected by people for assisting three generations of emperors, laying a solid foundation for future national prosperity. In her second half of life, her status was supreme to such an extent that she could even equate Empress Wu Zetian in terms of both power and reputation. She must have thought about her mausoleum when she was alive. According to the strict imperial system of Qing Dynasty, common burial place was called tomb; only the emperor's tomb can be called mausoleum, and only the empress could be buried in the mausoleum with the emperor. She was only a concubine who had not even been favored by Hong Taiji, inferior to her sister in status and even the two concubines of Ligdan Khan. While she excelled as a distinguished figure, she certainly was not willing to be buried together with those inferior concubines. She finally decided to bury herself nearby with such an excuse, "Your father (Hong Taiji) has been buried for a long time, so do not open the underground palace and disturb his rest. I miss you two (Emperor Shunzhi and Emperor Kangxi), and I do not want to be far away from you." Emperor Kangxi was very filial and obeyed her will. However, he did not select and build for her a resting tomb when he definitely had the capacity. It may be due to the dilemma between ancestral rituals and his grandmother's will, which made him feel hard to decide. As the most powerful woman in history of China, Emperor Wu Zetian did not even build a mausoleum for her, while Concubine Zhuang asked her grandson to build a separate mausoleum for her,

from which we can tell that Concubine Zhuang was actually a woman of ruse. Therefore there is West Zhaoling Imperial Tomb inside Shanhai Pass, so far away from the emperor, which is different from East or West Mausoleums. It is said that there is an empty tomb in Noble Concubines Garden, which are guessed to be prepared for Zhuang Concubine. It can said that Concubine Zhuang created a new system in Qing Dynasty, because no mausoleum was built for an empress before the time of Concubine Zhuang.

Speaking of Empress' mausoleums, we have to mention East Xiao Mausoleum, where is the graveyard of Emperor Shunzhi's Empress and concubines: Empress Xiaohuizhang and 28 concubines, attendant ladies and noble ladies. After completion of East Xiao Mausoleum, it was first called Xin Mausoleum, which was not officially named by the Court. When Empress Xiaohuizhang was buried into the underground palace, it was renamed as "Empress Xiaohuizhang's Mausoleum;" till fifty-eighth year of Emperor Kangxi (1718), Board of Rites reported to the throne, "Since ancient times, if Emperor and his Empress weren't buried together in one tomb, the name of Empress mausoleum shall be determined by its orientation towards the Emperor's. Now that Empress Xiaohuizhang's Mausoleum is on the east of Xiao Mausoleum, we do not have to find another name. We here draw up 'East Xiao Mausoleum' for your majesty to decide." Emperor Kangxi agreed this proposal, and since then, Empress Xiaohuizhang's Mausoleum was officially called East Xiao Mausoleum. The Mausoleum has the characteristics of Noble Concubines Garden, because many concubines were buried here. West Zhaoling Imperial Tomb is truly independent mausoleum for Empress. According to historical materials, there are also records regarding to building mausoleum for Concubine Zhuang, especially the issue of naming, which demonstrates that Qing Dynasty didn't have a mature mausoleum system. They had to follow the example of previous dynasties, i.e., an empress could also have a separate mausoleum, but it was still required to name the mausoleum after emperor's name and bore the orientation towards the emperor. Hong Taiji was buried in Zhaoling Imperial Tomb, so Concubine Zhuang's mausoleum was called West Zhaoling Imperial Tomb. West here refers to the direction judging from Shenyang. But East Qing Mausoleum and West Qing Mausoleum are named based on the directions judging from Beijing, just as East Mausoleum and North Mausoleum in Shenyang. Another example is Empress Xiaoshengxian, Emperor Yongzheng's empress, whose mausoleum is East Tai Mausoleum, located about 1.5 kilometers northwest of Tai Mausoleum, Emperor Yongzheng's tomb. There is also a special case that mother of Prince Gong Yixin was granted as an empress by Emperor Xianfeng after her death, so in Noble Concubines Garden, her tomb was added with walls for separation as a mausoleum.

Historically speaking, Empress Xiaoduanwen who had a calm character, feminine Hailanzhu or tough Concubine Zhuang are all great women and prides of Mongolian people. Concubine Zhuang also set an example for the later Empress Dowager Cixi who had also assisted three emperors: Xianfeng, Tongzhi and her sister's son Guangxu. Empress Wu Zetian had first killed her daughter and then her son in order to gain power, while Concubine Zhuang and Empress Dowager Cixi only attended to state affairs, which is clearly different with Empress Wu Zetian.

贵妃园出土的骨灰罐（现存隆恩殿神龛后）／左页图
Cinerary Jar Unearthed in Noble Concubines Garden (Kept behind Niche of Eminent Favor Hall) / Left Page

昭西陵庄妃宝城／上图
Burial Bastion for Concubine Zhuang in West Zhao Mausoleum / Upper

Even memorial tablet of Concubine Zhuang, mother of Emperor Shunzhi and one of the most powerful women in history, couldn't be put inside West Side-hall. In fact, West Side-hall was used for lamas (Mongolian Buddhist monks) to chant sutras and redeem lost souls by making offerings and saying prayers. Nurhaci believed in Lamaism when he was alive, and when Hong Taiji ruled, he also accorded great importance to the religion in order to win Mongolian nobles over. Jurchen's original religious belief was Shamanism, but later they changed to Lamaism for needs of politics and intermarriages, which was conducive to unite Mongolia, Qinghai and Tibet. Yonghe Temple in Beijing is originally Prince Yong's Mansion, and former residence of Emperor Yongzheng before his reign and also birth place of Emperor Qianlong. The Mansion was changed into Lama Temple in the 9th ruling year of Emperor Qianlong and became one of the country's highest level Buddhist temples. For the sake of Concubine Xiang, Emperor Qianlong also built a mosque in Summer Palace. The reason why emperors of Qing Dynasty highly honor Buddhism is clearly for national unity.

I find after a careful study that the roles of mausoleum buildings and the five palaces of Forbidden City are totally different. East Side-hall and West Sid-hall of Zhaoling Imperial Tomb flank on either side of the main hall in architectural layout, as its extensions and complementary parts. But East Side-hall and West Side-hall were not meant for memorial tablets of concubines as I thought before. That's also the reason behind fierce imperial conflicts and confrontations. Other imperial concubines were not even considered to be buried inside Square City, including Hong Taiji's favorite concubine, Hailanzhu, who was buried in Noble Concubines Garden. Common people might fight for emotions and properties, but imperial members had to experience life-and-death combats, and even struggles between family clans and interest groups, in oder to stamp their names on the page of history.

We once discovered a cremation jar inside Noble Concubines Garden, which made me feel overwhelmed by strong emotions on the spot. These imperial concubines might fight desperately for benefits and favor during their lifetime, but when they died; their remains were either gone or placed into a forgotten jar. Their names no longer arouse the slightest interest and attention of later generation, which is really pathetic. I put the jar inside Eminent Favor Hall for her ghost to reunite with Hong Taiji. The practice was not suitable according to conventions and rituals of Qing Dynasty, but there is indeed no place to put it.

东配楼／左页图
East Side-pavilion / Left Page
西配楼／下图
West Side-pavilion / Lower

被忽略的配楼

配楼是昭陵独有的建筑，也是昭陵在建筑上区别于福陵最大的一个特点，因为福陵里没有设置配楼。从这点上，可以看出昭陵比福陵的级别地位要高。但是很多人认为福陵与昭陵一样，忽略了拿配楼作参照物，很多学术著作里甚至不提及配楼，而很多摄影家也不重视昭陵配楼，都只关注隆恩殿等主要建筑。如果没有配楼，那么福陵与昭陵可能真是不好区分了。

我多年一直想把配楼拍好，因为有城墙阴影的缘故，多年未能如愿。而最近一次在昭陵拍摄时，由于午后光线很好，使我在方城的马道上拍摄隆恩门内东边的配楼时，得到了非常满意的作品，感谢天赐。还遇到一位摄影爱好者，跟他探讨了一下摄影中的光影知识，高兴之余，还把多年的拍摄经验告诉他们，使他很感动，我也体会到助人的快乐。

西配楼／左页图
West Side-pavilion / Left Page

西配楼旧照／下图
Old Picture of West Side-pavilion / Lower

NEGLECTED SIDE PAVILION

Side Pavilion is a unique building of Zhaoling Imperial Tomb, which is a distinctive feature in comparison with Fu Mausoleum. As there is no such building in Fu Mausoleum, it can be seen that rank and position of Zhaoling Imperial Tomb is higher than Fu Mausoleum. The people who regard the two mausoleums as same actually neglect the existence of Side Pavilion. Many scholars fail to refer to Side Pavilion in their works, and many photographers mainly focus on taking photos of the main buildings such as Eminent Favor Hall, neglecting its existence.

However, if Side Pavilion is overlooked, differences between Zhaoling Imperial Tomb and Fu Mausoleum are rendered not easy to find.

I had made great endeavors to take some ideal pictures of Side Pavilion for years, but always failed due to the shadow of wall. But during my latest trip, I got satisfactory pictures on a bright afternoon when I photoed East Side Pavilion inside Eminent Favor Gate. I also encountered a shutterbug, with whom I discussed photograph techniques and shared some of my pictures. He was really impressed by my tricks and grateful to learn something from me, while I savored great happiness of helping others.

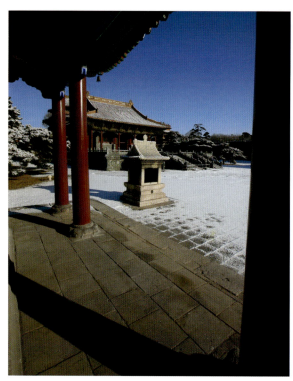
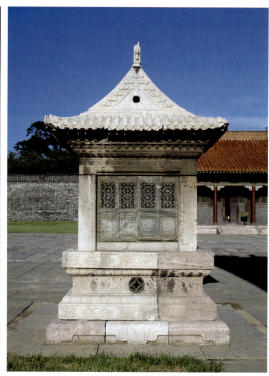

阴阳两界的邮局
——焚帛亭

焚帛亭坐落在隆恩殿西南，是一座用汉白玉雕制的小型亭子式建筑。亭子内为"火池"，是大祭时用来焚烧彩纸和金箔、银箔等祭品的，按照大祭礼仪，每次大祭要给皇帝、皇后烧纸1万张，金、银箔1万锭。给妃、嫔、贵人每人烧三色纸1千张，金银箔1千锭。给常在、福晋、格格每人烧素纸1千张，金银箔1千锭。皇帝东巡大祭时观看焚化祭品全过程，以尽孝道，称为"望燎"，是大祭最后一道程序。亭子的下部是须弥座，上下有檐，中间凹进去，有缩腰，座上还刻有各式花纹，整个亭子造型十分精致、细腻。这座小巧洁白的亭子也成为金碧辉煌的陵寝建筑的一个点缀。这样一个小亭子，似乎是沟通阴阳两界的邮局，活着的人将自己的哀思寄托于彩纸、金箔、银箔等祭品，烧给另一个世界的人。

这不由让我想到了永陵焚帛亭，比较简陋，只是青砖铁门。而福陵的焚帛亭也与昭陵不同，它有上檐而无下檐，显然下面的一部分被掩埋在土里了，那么这究竟是自身下陷的，还是被后人埋进去的呢？它究竟是完整的底座，还是半截的，一直让我费解。关外三陵的焚帛亭与关内清陵的焚帛亭相比，名字上略有不同，关内都称之为焚帛炉，功能却都一致，只是关内的焚帛炉更加精致而华丽，每座焚帛炉都是用琉璃镶嵌的封闭式小型建筑，而关外的焚帛亭相比之下，只有四根柱子和亭檐，是四面敞口的开放式小亭，显得有点过于简陋了。

焚帛亭
Silk-burning Pavilion

SILK-BURNING PAVILION — POST OFFICE BETWEEN LIFE AND DEATH

Silk-burning Pavilion is located to the southwest of Eminent Favor Hall, which is a small building carved out of white marble. Inside the pavilion is a "fire pit" burning colorful paper, gold and silver foils (made of silk or papers) and other offerings in grand sacrifices. In accordance with grand sacrificial rituals, there should be ten thousand pieces of paper money and ten thousand golden and silver foils burnt for emperor and empress on grand sacrifices. One thousand pieces of paper money and one thousand pieces of golden and silver foils should be burnt for concubines and court ladies. One thousand pieces of plain paper and one thousand pieces of golden and silver foils should be burnt for call ladies, noble ladies and attendant ladies. It is the last procedure of grand sacrifices when Emperor watches the whole process of burning sacrificial offerings to show his filial piety during his eastern tour for worship, which is called "Burning Watch." The lower part of the pavilion is a Sumeru throne, with eaves on its upper and lower parts and its middle recessed, forming a thinner waist. Its throne is carved with various patterns and designs. The whole pavilion modeling is delicate and fine in sculpture, and therefore the pavilion is always deemed as a highlight of the resplendent and magnificent Mausoleum. This little pavilion is like a post office between life and death, delivering griefs and missings of the living to the deceased by burning such sacrificial offering as colorful papers, gold and silver foils.

The sight of this Silk-burning Pavilion reminds me of the one in Yong Mausoleum, which is simply made of grey bricks with iron cast door. However, in contrast with the one in Zhaoling Imperial Tomb, Silk-burning Pavilion of Fu Mausoleum only has upper eaves while traces of its lower eaves can't be found. Apparently its lower part has been buried underneath. How did that occurred? Did it sink by itself or was it buried by others? Is the buried part a complete throne or only a segment? It is indeed a puzzle requiring further study. Silk-burning Pavilions of Three Mausoleums outside Shanhai Pass are slightly different in name from those inside the Pass, which are called Silk-burning Stoves. Both the Pavilions and the Stoves have the same functions, but Silk-burning Stoves inside the Pass are more gorgeously decorated and delicate. Each Silk-burning Stove is of small glazed enclosed structure while Silk-burning Pavilion is a simple pavilion with four pillars, eaves and openings on its four sides.

清西陵（泰陵）东焚帛炉 / 左上图
East Silk-burner of West Qing Mausoleum (Tai Mausoleum) / Upper Left

清西陵（泰陵）西焚帛炉 / 右上图
West Silk-burner of West Qing Mausoleum (Tai Mausoleum) / Upper Right

昭西陵焚帛炉
青砖结构外贴琉璃 已毁 / 下图
Silk-burner with Grey-brick Structure Glazed outside in West Zhao Mausoleum, Destroyed / Lower

焚帛亭 / 右页图
Silk-burning Pavilion / Right Page

石五供／左页图
Stone Five Offerings / Left Page

二柱门／下图
Dual Pillar Gate / Lower

人无路，魂有道的二柱门

在隆恩殿须弥座与石五供之间，有一座牌坊式的栅栏门，两扇门勉强可以打开，门南北两面真是无路可言。因门两边各有一方形石柱，而被称作"二柱门"。柱子的顶端各有一"望天犼"（注解12），而令人觉得奇怪的是，它们的腿上竟被拴上了条铁链，相传这犼吸收了日月之精华，竟然成精，不再安分守己，因此便用铁链控制住它。

然而这扇门却是有名无实，常年关闭，而且从功能上讲是不能供来往行人出入的。而永陵却是没有二柱门的，只不过在启运殿后墙上挖了个洞，那昭陵这扇门到底为何存在？又有着怎样的意义呢？"人无路，魂有道"，其实，二柱门是给灵魂走的。可以回想百年之前，在皇宫大院内，自由是一件多么奢侈的事情，对于掌握天下的皇帝来说尚且如此，更外乎那些红墙内的寻常官员抑或妃嫔宫婢呢？想当年乾隆皇帝多次微服出巡，大概不单单是为了体察民情，也有自身想出去走走的一小部分原因吧。话说乾隆曾经微服出巡，路过一家烧麦铺，吃过后大加赞赏，提名"都一处"，之后，这家小店的生意一直兴旺至今。

皇家陵园设计中多含暗喻，例如沈阳故宫中只有一个烟囱，寓意一"筒"天下，在这里，二柱门的存在也有它自己的道理。既然活着的时候自由已经如此难求，那就让红墙内的灵魂可以自由出入，一偿夙愿吧。二柱门是留给灵魂出入的地方，是纯礼制性的建筑，没有实用价值。道光帝慕陵以后开始不设置。而慕陵里不仅没有二柱门、神功圣德碑、月牙城等，甚至也没有风水红墙，而是灰黄交融的墙垣，也没有宝城，可以说是清陵中规制较小却比较独特的陵寝。慕陵，取仰慕祖陵之意，而当时也正值清朝走向衰亡的时期，可能其中也流露着道光帝乃至整个大清朝都对以往"康乾盛世"鼎盛时代的深切怀念与重建的深深期望吧。而清代帝王及皇后们，都是非常谦虚的，当他们觉得自己的功绩不如先祖，或某些地方愧对先祖，他们往往在陵寝建筑上也将自己的自责和愧疚之情体现出来。他们不仅仅删减礼制建筑，还将风水墙的红色换成灰黄色，隆恩殿内不装饰彩绘，就连慈禧陵寝也同样体现出这种谦逊的态度。有人也许会提出反驳，并举出慈禧陵寝隆恩殿突雕的手法使"凤在上龙在下"的例子。其实，那是大家的偏见而已，如果到离慈禧陵寝只有一墙之隔的东太后慈安的陵寝看一看，就会发现同样是"凤在上而龙在下"。我想，那只是体现出当时清朝的"凤为母，龙为子"的一种现实。

DUAL PILLAR GATE — SPIRITS PATH OF THE DEAD RATHER THAN FOR THE LIVING

Between the Sumeru base of Eminent Favor Hall and Stone Five Offerings is a Memorial arch-like barrier gate, doors of which can be barely opened. The gate has impasses both on its south and north. There is a square stone pillar on either side of the gate and therefore it is called "Dual Pillar Gate." On top of either pillar, there is a "Sky-roaring Hou" (see Note 12). To our surprise, their legs are bound with chains. It is said that "Hou" had absorbed radiances of the sun and the moon and become spirits. They had to be chained because they often acted badly.

However, this gate is only a nominal one, for it remains closed throughout the year. What's more, it can't be used by pedestrians functionally. Yong Mausoleum has no gate like this, but a hole on the back wall of Qiyun Hall (Luck-provoking Hall). So what is the purpose of such a gate? Does it have any symbolic meaning? Dual Pillar Gate is actually a path for spirits of the deceased rather than for the living. Dating back to the feudal society over a hundred years ago, we can find that freedom was nothing but a luxury and wild wish even for emperors, let alone those ordinary officials or concubines. Emperor Qianlong often privately visited people, not simply to experience and observe ordinary people's lives, but also to enjoy solitary travel. It is said that Emperor Qianlong once passed through a steamed pork dumpling restaurant and sang high praise for the food there. He left his own handwriting "Du Yi Chu," and the restaurant's business has been prosperous till now.

Design of the imperial mausoleums contains a lot of implications. Take Imperial Palace of Shenyang for example, whose only chimney implies unification of the whole world (as in Chinese "tong" in "烟筒" meaning "chimney" is a homophone of "tong" in "统一" meaning "unification"). Dual Pillar Gate is also justifiable here with its own implied meaning. Freedom was too difficult to get for the living inside the imperial palace, so a gate was built for their souls here in the mausoleum, symbolizing grant of freedom after they went to heaven. The Gate, where spirits enter and exit, is a purely ritual building without any practical value. The Gate didn't stop existing until Emperor Daoguang's Mu Mausoleum, in which there were not built Dual Pillar Gate, Stele of Divine Merits, Crescent City, Burial Bastion, and even red geomantic walls (only grey yellowish walls), a small-scale but quite unique mausoleum. "Mu" means "admire" in Chinese, from which we can see Emperor Daoguang's lingering on "Prosperity of Kangxi and Qianlong" and his expectation of its revival and reconstruction, because Qing Dynasty was then declining and falling. The emperors and empresses in Qing Dynasty were so modest and humble that they expressed their self-blame and guilt in the construction of their mausoleums when they thought they were not good as their ancestors in political achievements. They reduced rituals and number of buildings, replaced red with grey and yellow on geomantic walls, and decorated no colorful paintings in the Eminent Favor Hall. Even Empress Cixi's mausoleum also showed this kind of humility. One might doubt and propose the example of the embossment of "Phoenix on top and Dragon below" in Eminent Favor Hall of Cixi's mausoleum, which, in fact, is only our prejudice: if you just walk for a look into Empress Cian's tomb, a wall away from the mausoleum of Cixi, you will find it is the same case of "Phoenix on the top and Dragon under below." In my view, it just reflects the idea of "Phoenix for mother and Dragon for child" in Qing Dynasty.

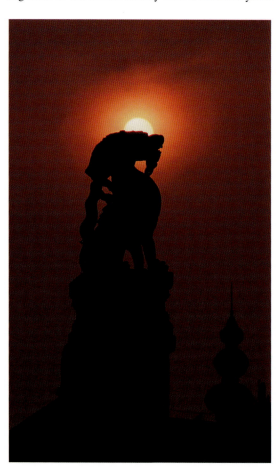

石五供（从宝城门望石五供）
Stone Five Offerings, Seen from Gate of Burial Bastion

不朽的供桌
——石五供

石祭台在二柱门之后，用汉白玉雕刻，这祭台之上供奉有五件石雕：正中为香炉（又叫海山），两侧有香瓶、烛台各一对，因此也叫"石五供"。只有道光帝慕陵内的石五供由内到外依次是香炉、石蜡台和石花瓶。炉中立有"紫石火焰"，石花瓶上也立有紫石，取香烟不断，烛火长明，大清江山万代之意。福陵石花瓶和石烛台上的实物已经丢失了，昭陵石花瓶上的两块紫石尚存。由此我不由得想到了李白的诗句"日照香炉生紫烟"，诗中提到的"紫烟"并不是紫色的烟，而是象征着紫气东来的祥瑞之气，与石五供上的紫石寓意暗合。石五供对民国时期总统的陵寝建筑有着很深的影响，不论是袁世凯墓，还是张作霖的元帅林都有石五供，只是元帅林内没有石祭台，把石五供直接放在了地面上。这里是古代大祭时皇帝在此哀悼和献祭之处。有时，我也困惑，为什么殿内有祭祀用的香炉，而在此处还有设置一个石头的祭台，其意义何在？我至今还没想明白。而永陵中并没有石五供，福陵昭陵中却都设置了。

福陵和昭陵内隆恩殿、二柱门、石五供距离很近，近到行人都无法通行的地步。而清东陵、清西陵三者之间的距离要远得多，在隆恩殿后面还有陵寝门，是三座琉璃花门，它们是整个陵寝前朝和后寝的分界线。

昭西陵石五供／上图
Stone Five Offerings in West Zhao Mausoleum / Upper
昭陵石五供／下图
Stone Five Offerings in Zhao Mausoleum / Lower
石五供——海山／右页图
Haishan (Literally means "seamount", an joss stick furnace in the middle of Stone Five Offerings) / Right Page

LONGLASTING ALTAR — STONE FIVE OFFERINGS

A stone altar lies behind Dual Pillar Gate, carved out of white marble. Five stone carvings, or "Stone Five Offerings," are placed on the altar: an joss stick furnace in the middle (also called "Haishan" meaning "seamount"), with a pair of incense vases and candlestick holders on its either side respectively. Only in Mu Mausoleum of Emperor Daoguang are Stone Five Offerings arranged in the sequence of incense furnace, stone incense holders and stone incense vases from inside to outside. In the furnace, there are "purple stone flames," and on top of the stone vases, implying continuous burning of joss sticks and candles, and blessing for the territory of Qing Dynasty. The items on the stone holders and vases in Fu Mausoleum have been lost, while purple stones on the vases remain in Zhaoling Imperial Tomb, from which I could not help thinking of Li Bai's poem "The sunlit censer exhales a wreath of purple mist," "Zi Yan" (purple mist) here doesn't refer to purple mist, but a symbol of good fortune, which matches the implied meaning of purple stones on Stone Five Offerings. Stone Five Offerings also have deep influence on Presidents' mausoleum construction in the Republican Period; Stone Five Offerings can be found in both Yuan Shikai's tomb and Marshal Zhang Zuolin's woods; one difference is that in Zhang's tomb, no stone altar was built and Stone Five Offerings were directly placed on the ground. Here is the place where emperors mourned and offered their sacrifices on grand sacrificial ceremonies. Sometimes, this extra stone altar puzzles me considering the existence of an incense burner for sacrifices inside Eminent Favor Hall. And I am still not clear why both Zhaoling

Imperial Tomb and Fu Mausoleum have Stone Five Offerings while Yong Mausoleum doesn't have.

In Fu or Zhaoling Imperial Tomb, the distances between Eminent Favor Hall, Double Pillar Gate and Stone Five Offerings are too close for people to pass through. But the distances between these three buildings inside East or West Qing Mausoleum are much farther. And in the back of Eminent Favor Hall, there are also mausoleum gates, which are three color-glazed gates, a boundary line of the entire mausoleum's front and rear parts.

大明楼／上图
Grand Ming Tower / Upper
大明楼与宝顶／右图
Grand Ming Tower and Blessed Vault / Right

多灾多难大明楼

大明楼坐落于方城北门上，前檐挂有匾额，用满、蒙、汉三种文体写着"昭陵"二字。在大明楼内立有一通汉白玉石碑，碑头为龙首，正中开光部分刻有"昭陵"，碑身刻有"太宗文皇帝之陵"字样，碑身四周篆刻着精细的游龙纹，碑座为须弥座，此碑叫作"圣号碑"。碑身上所刻的是皇太极的庙号和谥号。庙号是皇帝死后，被立室奉祀时所赐予的名号，形式多是表示为某祖某宗，如太祖、太宗。谥号是皇帝、后妃、王公、大臣、贵族及士大夫死后，根据他们生前的品行和事迹，给他们评定的称号，是对这个人一生浓缩了的评价。

大明楼是整个昭陵最高的建筑，"树大招风"，这座楼在历史上几次遭受雷火袭击，最严重的一次是在伪满康德四年（1936年），大明楼几乎被雷火烧毁，1931年"九·一八事变"后，整个中国都生灵涂炭，大明楼也未能幸免，而现在的大明楼是于1939年重修的。

大明楼石碑旧照／左上图
Old Picture of Stele of Grand Ming Tower / Upper Left
昭西陵孝庄文皇后之陵碑／右上图
Gravestone for Empress Xiaozhuangwen in West Zhao Mausoleum / Upper Right
大明楼石碑／右页图
Stele of Grand Ming Tower / Right Page

CALAMITOUS GRAND MING TOWER

Grand Ming Tower (Daminglou in Chinese pronunciation, the tall building right in front of the tomb) lies on top of the northern gate of Square City. Its front eave has a board inscribed with characters "Zhaoling Imperial Tomb" in Manchu, Mongolian, and Chinese. Inside the Tower, there is a white marble stone tablet, top of which is inscribed with dragons flying around "Zhaoling Imperial Tomb" inscribed in its consecrated middle. The body of the tablet is inscribed with characters "Mausoleum of Emperor Taizongwen," while its periphery is inscribed with delicate designs of dragon swimming in the water, and its base is of Sumeru throne. This kind of stone tablet is called "Emperor Title tablet." What were carved on the tablet are the name of temple and the posthumous title of Hong Taiji. Temple name is the title offered in receiving the enshrinement after an emperor's death, which is mostly expressed as X Tsu and X Zong, such as Tai Tsu and Tai Zong. Posthumous title is the title offered by appraising their lifelong conducts and deeds after the death of Emperor, Empress, nobility, ministers, aristocrats and literati, which is the condensed evaluation of this person's whole life.

Grand Ming Tower is the highest building of the whole Zhaoling Imperial Tomb. "A tall tree invites the wind" (which is used to symbolize "A person with great reputation is liable to be attacked.") This building has suffered from lightning strikes a couple of times. The most serious strike took place at the 4th year of Kangde of Manchu State (1936), in which the Tower was nearly burned down with the thunder. After "September 18 Incident" in 1931, China was plunged into an abyss of misery and destruction, and the Tower was no exception with a complete demolish. The existing Grand Ming Tower was actually restored later in 1939.

数理与昭陵风水

在昭陵陵寝里，有很多数字是值得推敲的。一般古代建筑上的数字，阳宅是奇数，也叫阳数，阴宅是偶数，也叫阴数。作为皇家建筑来讲，宫殿最大的是9，王府一般是7，逐级往下排列，但是作为建筑台阶数量来讲，就是3级、5级、7级、9级台阶。有个小故事，乾隆和豫亲王下棋，豫亲王棋艺很高，但总是输给乾隆，乾隆想分出个真正的胜负，就想出个主意，下棋输赢的赌注，就是赢门钉。如果皇帝赢了，则拔豫亲王家门上的一颗钉，如果豫亲王赢了则把豫亲王家的围墙增加一尺。皇帝输了也不赏赐门钉，因为赏一颗门钉就变偶数是阴宅了，而赏两颗就9颗，就和皇宫一样了，属于越制了。由此可见古代门钉数的重要。一般只有阴宅用偶数，最大的数用8，但也有特殊的现象，比如太和殿是10，行10，京，是大房子的意思，是只有皇帝才能住的，太和殿在当时是北京最大的建筑，但是10是偶数。还有紫禁城的东华门，是一行8个门钉，是皇帝驾崩的时候，出入梓棺的专用通道，所以阴宅阳宅不是用一个简单的理论就能涵盖所有的。

昭陵在建筑的数理上，是非常值得研究的一门学问。先说门钉吧，昭陵正红门扇正反两面都有门钉，而福陵正红门上没有门钉。现在昭陵正红门门钉个数正面最多一行6个，反面最多一行是7个，隆恩门正面最多一行8个，反面一行是9个，月牙城门正面最多一行6个，反面最多一行也是6个。由此可见，清昭陵的门，是区分阴阳两界的门。同一扇门，似乎进代表阴界，出则代表阳界。但是，我查看了当年的老照片，发现昭陵正红门的门钉原来正反两面都是9个的，而关内清陵门钉一般也都是9个，这既和古代阴宅阳宅的道理不同，和现在的阴阳两界分割的理论也不一致。究竟什么原因，现在已经无人知晓，无据可考。到了月牙城，皇帝只在石五供前哭祭，并不进城。再说吻兽的数量，昭陵隆恩殿殿脊上的吻兽数是5个，东西配殿吻兽是3个。

影壁上的牡丹值得深究，在清皇朝的历史上，共有12位皇帝，恰好与墙上的12朵牡丹相契合，是一种简单的数字巧合，抑或是一种意蕴深长的历史暗示，抑或真是风水？用浪漫主义的想象来看，这面墙真算得上是清朝的缩影，十二牡丹象征了12位皇帝令人瞩目的一生，也象征了12位皇帝所经历的兴衰荣辱，果真是一墙看尽繁华如梦，历史如烟。这种巧合同样也出现在永陵之中，人们将永陵中启运山错落起伏的山峰与清朝国势联系起来，据说这每个山峰的高度恰好与清朝从古至今的12位皇帝的命数相契合，位于中间的山峰最高象征康乾盛世，而第十二个几乎看不出来是座山峰，注定第十二个皇帝为亡国之君。这究竟是百姓民间人为附会的传说，抑或单单是历史的巧合，都是我们无法辨识的了。但我知道，这个世界上就是有一些巧合是无法言喻的，学者各有信仰，而信仰与科学往往并存，牛顿在晚年不也将"第一推动"归于了上帝吗？我在《文昌祖庭》中谈到过的"天聋地哑"（注解13），它们所蕴含的公正秉直之意也是后人附会的，只是这样的理解也无伤大雅，相反还会更有意思，因而被流传了下来。

地宫影壁墙 / 左页图
Screen Wall of Underground Palace / Left Page
昭西陵宝城没有影壁 / 上图
Burial Bastion without Screen Wall in West Zhao Mausoleum / Upper
清东陵孝陵影壁 / 下图
Screen Wall of East Qing Mausoleum / Lower

NUMBER AND ZHAOLING IMPERIAL TOMB FENGSHUI (GEOMANCY)

Many numbers of Zhaoling Imperial Tomb need our attention and consideration. Generally speaking, in ancient Chinese architectural buildings, odd numbers are found in buildings for the living, while even numbers are used in tombs and mausoleums. Among imperial buildings, imperial palace can use the number 9 symbolizing the highest rank, prince mansion uses 7, and other buildings with smaller odd numbers. And 3-step, 5-step, 7-step and 9-step stairs are built for people of different social castes. There is a story about Emperor Qianlong and Enfante Rong, both of whom loved playing Chinese chess. Although Enfante Rong played better, he always pretended he was a lousy player and lost to Emperor Qianlong all the time. So in order to play fair, Emperor Qianlong thought over and proposed doornails as stake, i.e. if Enfante Rong lost, one doornail would be pulled out from his mansion gate. But if he won, he could heighten his walls one chi (Chinese traditional unit of length, equal to 1/3 meter). However, doornails of Enfante Rong's gate couldn't be added more than 9, otherwise it would be considered violation of feudal rituals, so an alternative of heightening walls was introduced. But if Emperor Qianlong lost, doornails of imperial palace would not be pulled out, because even number was used only on tombs. So significance of number of doornails could be verified in the story. Generally speaking, tomb buildings used even number with 8 as the biggest one, but exception did exist. For example, Taihe Hall (Supreme Harmony Hall) adopts the even number 10. Number 10 refers to grand houses, in which only emperors can live, and Taihe Hall was then the biggest building in Beijing. In addition, East Hua Gate of Forbidden City has 8 doornails in a row, which is actually a special path for coffins of deceased emperors. The odd and even number rule was usually observed, but sometimes there might be some exceptional cases.

Number of items in Zhaoling Imperial Tomb is something that needs our further study. For instance, doors of Zhaoling Imperial Tomb have nails on their both sides, while those of Fu Mausoleum only have nails on their front sides. The front side of Front Red Gate has 6 nails at most in a row, and 7 nails at most in a row on its back, while the front of Eminent Favor Gate has 8 nails at most in a row, and 9 nails at most in a row on its back. The door of Crescent City has 6 nails at most in a row on its front and 7 on its back. From these numbers, we can see that doors of Zhaoling Imperial Tomb are regarded as dividing line of life and death. It seems coming inside the door symbolizes entering the world of the dead, and walking out means stepping into the world of the living. However, when I examined their old photos, I found that the numbers of doornails on the front and back sides of Front Red Gate in Zhaoling Imperial Tomb are both 9, the same numbers as the ones in mausoleums inside the Pass, which is quite different from ancient theory about houses for the dead and the living, and the present dichotomy of yin (dead) and yang (living). Nobody know why now and we have no evidence to study further. In Crescent City, emperors only offered their sacrifices in front altar of Stone Five Offerings rather than went inside. Number of Wenshou (Kissing animal, an animal structure at the ends of a roof ridge) also indicates imperial rituals, for example there are 5 wenshous on the ridge of Eminent Favor Hall, but only 3 on that of East Side-hall and West Side-hall respectively.

Peonies on Screen Wall are well worth research. In the history of Qing Dynasty, there were altogether 12 emperors, identical with the number of peonies on the Wall. Is it a simple coincidence or a purposeful design with profound historical hint? In a romantic way, this wall seems like a miniature of Qing Dynasty: The twelve peonies symbolize twelve emperors' rise and recession. The same coincidence of number "12" also exists in Yong Mausoleum, on whose Screen Wall 12 peaks are said to be related with the fate of Qing Dynasty emperors with each representing one emperor. The highest peak in the middle symbolizes prosperity of Emperors Kangxi and Qianlong's Period, while the 12th, which is almost invisible, symbolizes doom of the 12th emperor's fate. We have no way to judge if it is a legend or a historical coincidence. There are some unexplainable facts in the world, and even scholars have their religious beliefs together with their scientific view. For instance, the great scientist Newton attributed the first driving force of the earth to God. The implied meaning of integrity and uprightness by "Heavenly deaf and earthly dumb" (see Note 13) mentioned in Wenchang Ancestral Courts was also added by later generation. Such kind of understanding is not harmful but instead interesting, and thus accepted by later generation.

清东陵孝陵方城 / 下图
Square City of East Qing Mausoleum / Lower

夕照月牙城 / 右页图
Crescent City in Sunset / Right Page

清东陵被盗"逼走"溥仪

说到盗墓，我不由联想到辽墓的"十墓九空"。女真对于契丹是恨之入骨的，契丹对女真的迫害不仅表现在侵城略地，甚至强抢民女，像英格兰贵族在侵略苏格兰时蛮横剥夺少女的初夜权一样，妄图改变种族，这种仇恨是难以泯灭的。于是，在女真族攻下契丹族的大辽之后，辽墓就出现了这种状况，一洗前耻的女真部落纷纷挖坟掘墓，对辽人之墓进行了大规模的破坏，是一种报复式的精神胜利法。挖坟掘墓可以说是中国朝代更迭中的一个特色。最早的伍子胥掘墓，鞭尸楚平王，这里体现的是一种恨，元对西夏最狠，掘墓者甚至在攻城时将墓烧毁，在破城时命人将墓碑一块块砸得粉碎。而满族则不同，清朝入关以后，甚至连多尔衮的墓都被挫骨扬灰，却并没有掘明朝的祖坟。照理说，明朝杀了努尔哈赤的父亲，皇太极的爷爷，清朝应该对其深恶痛绝，挖坟掘墓，但是说清朝伟大正是伟大在这一点上。清朝采取了一种宽容的态度，融合各个民族，而并非单靠武力来统一中国。因为，清朝帝王认为自己是真正的华夏继承者。所以说，清的民族政策历来最好，国民政府则反之，末代皇帝溥仪投靠日本帝国主义并不仅是因为被驱逐出皇宫和日本的威逼利诱，最终激怒他的直接原因是当时的民国掘了清东陵，掘了祖坟，这样的羞辱不仅仅是针对溥仪一个人的，也是整个民族的悲哀，正因如此，溥仪最终决定反抗，投靠了日本帝国主义，走上了最终的傀儡之路。最让我印象深刻的是，东京审判里，有人问溥仪：伪满洲国皇帝有个人行动自由吗？溥仪沉默了一会儿说："所谓'自由'一词，十几年中与我毫无关系，简直就是猴戏。"一句如此平静的话，却引出了我心中悲伤的波澜，生在如此的境遇之中，只是不断被从一个牢笼中转移到另一个牢笼中，虽有心复国，却终不得志，活在别人的操纵之下，又怎能拥有属于自己的天空？

不停流逝的时间并没有断绝人们奇谲的幻想。月牙城是一个有故事的地方，这座沧桑的建筑会带着它的故事，一直缄默地等下去，直到有一天，人们能够真正揭开它的面纱。

昭西陵没有月牙城，上城的通道是从内部通向楼顶的 / 上图
There is no Crescent City in West Zhao Mausoleum, and the Passage up to City Wall is accessible from inside / Upper

月牙城 / 右图
Crescent City / Right

EXCAVATION OF EAST QING MAUSOLEUM, THE REASON WHY PU YI BECAME PUPPET EMPEROR

Talking about grave robbers, I could not help thinking about the imperial tombs of Liao Dynasty, which are described as "Nine out of ten are empty." Jurchen's hatred for the Khitan is in depth. Khitan people intruded on Jurchen and robbed their women. Like nobles of England, when they invaded Scotland, they wanted droit du seigneur of the local maidens and intended to change their ethnicity. This is an ineradicable great hatred difficult to forgive. Therefore, after their capture of Khitan's Liao, Jurchen excavated Khitan's tombs and destroyed them in order to make their revenge, which was actually a kind of spiritual victory. Excavation of tombs is a feature typical of China in the succession of dynasties. At the earliest time, Wu Zixu opened King's tomb of Chu State and whipped his body as an expression of hatred. The hatred of Yuan Dynasty for Western Xia is even worse. Those grave robber even burned their tombs and smashed their steles into pieces. Differently, Manchu did not even revenge, and instead kept the tombs of Ming Dynasty despite the fact that Dorgon's tomb was destroyed. As Ming Dynasty killed Nurhaci's father, i.e. Hong Taiji's grandfather, it was taken for granted that Qing would destroy emperor tombs of Ming. That's what made Qing Dynasty so great – a tolerant attitude, which promoted ethnic unification more than conquering by force. The rulers of Qing Dynasty had already regarded themselves as the successor of Great China. Therefore, Qing's ethnic policy is the best in history. On the contrary, the government of Republic of China acted another way. Pu Yi, the last emperor of Qing Dynasty turned to Japan not because of being expelled out of the palace or coercion of Japan, but because the government of Republic of China dug Eastern Qing Mausoleum – his ancestors' grave, which is a shame for Pu Yi, also a shame of the whole Chinese nation. Pu Yi was forced to step into the way of being a puppet emperor. I was deeply impressed with Pu Yi's answer at Tokyo trial, "Do you have freedom as Emperor of Manchu State?" Keeping silent for a while, Pu Yi said, "The word 'freedom' has nothing to do with me over ten years. I was controlled as in a monkey show." Such a remark elicited sorrows from my heart. Living under his miserable circumstances, he was just being a caged bird. He could not achieve his ambition, even though he wanted to dedicate his life to his country. Living under other people's control, how could he have his own sky?

The nonstopping time invites people's imagination of different kinds to Crescent City. The historical mysterious building awaits there, together with all its ups and downs, hoping one day in the future people can unveil its stories.

月牙城还是哑巴院？

"人有悲欢离合，月有阴晴圆缺"，苏轼的一首《水调歌头》，咏出了月与人之间情感的一种微妙契合，月缺有悲伤离散之意。望文生义，月牙城正是这样一个凭吊先皇，寄托哀思的地方，也是整个陵寝中极富浪漫色彩的院落。

形如新月之状的月牙城，是方城与宝城之间出现的一个特殊空间，这个小小院落的北墙上嵌着一个琉璃影壁，上面镌刻着盛放的牡丹，花叶交错，精致而华贵。凝视着这面美丽异常的影壁，任谁都会徒生出一些奇妙的想象，有的人就认为，这面墙壁后暗藏着打开地宫的秘密通道，拧动墙上图案中的某一块，就是打开了机关，神秘的地宫便会浮出水面……当然，这种电影般的情节并没有发生在月牙城内，几百年来风雨不动的沉默让它一直笼罩在一种猜不透的朦胧之中。

清代陵寝中，关内陵寝一般都有月牙城和宝城，除了道光帝的慕陵。与关外三陵不同的是，关内陵寝的宝城一般都是整圆形，月牙向内，而关外宝城却是半圆形，月牙向外，永陵宝城特殊点，呈八角弧形。有关月牙城的传说也有些诡异，月牙城又称"哑巴院"，一说是当年修建地宫陵寝时，为防止工人们将皇陵地宫中的秘密泄露出去，引来盗墓之人，因而将所有的1000名工匠集中到院内，强制他们服下了一种毒药，致使他们全部失声，甚至将这些人封入地宫，成为地宫之中永远的殉葬者；一说是在修建地宫时只招哑巴作为工匠，因为皇宫幽深，隐藏着无穷的秘密，而能够接触这些秘密，唯一的要求就是永远保持沉默，有口而不能言。究竟这"哑巴院"的传说从何而来，也成了一个不解之谜。而我认为，前一种说法的可能性不大，如果用某些手段将工匠全部毒哑，就必定会招致他们的记恨，就算不用语言，这些工匠们也一定会用手势或者文字抒发自己的不满，古时的人不会这样考虑不周的。

CRESCENT CITY OR DUMB COURTYARD?

"People have their joys and griefs, their togetherness and separation. The moon has its dark and clear times, its waxing and waning." The verse of famous poet Su Shi describes the subtle emotional conformity of moon with people in his poem Prelude to Water Melody. A waning moon implies departure and separation, and thus Crescent City is literally such a place for people to visit and ponder on the deceased emperors, and also a court tinted with romantic atmosphere.

Crescent City, shaped like a new crescent moon, is a special courtyard between Square City and Burial Bastion. The northern wall of the small courtyard is embedded with a screen wall of colored glaze. Screen Wall is carved with blooming peonies with interlaced flowers and leaves, looking delicate and luxurious. For its unusual beauty, fantasy and admiration will occur to whoever watches the Wall. Some people would fantasize that there is a secret passage to the underground palace of the Mausoleum, and that if you trigger some part of the design on Screen Wall, the mysterious underground palace will emerge… Certainly, the movie-like plot did not take place inside Crescent City, and it remained silent with a confusing haze for hundreds of years.

Of the mausoleums of Qing Dynasty inside the Shanhai Pass, there are Crescent Cities and Burial Bastions above the underground palace, but Mu Mausoleum of Daoguang Emperor is an exception. Burial Bastions inside the Pass are usually round-shaped with inward Crescents. In contrast, Burial Bastions outside the Pass are are semicircled with outward crescents. And what is typical the Bastion in Yong Mausoleum is its octagonal shape. Tales about Crescent City are somewhat mysterious and strange, as it is also called "Dumb Courtyard." One story follows that when the underground mausoleum was built, to prevent workers from revealing the secrets and then bringing in grave robbers, 1000 craftsmen were called to the courtyard and forced to take a poison, which made them dumb. They were even enclosed in the underground palace and buried there forever. Another story is that only dumb people were recruited as workers, so that hidden secrets inside the underground palace had no access to leak out. How on earth comes the name "Dumb Courtyard" remains a mystery. In my opinion, the first saying is unbelievable, because if they were poisoned to be made dumb, they would also express out their dissatisfaction with gestures or characters, even they could not speak, which the decision maker had to consider.

昭西陵宝城内部通道／下图
Interior Passage of Burial Bastion in West Zhao Mausoleum / Lower
月牙城与西北角楼／右页图
Crescent City and Northwest Turret / Right Page

宝顶神树 / 左页图
Divine Tree on Blessed Vault / Left Page
清西陵（慕陵）宝顶 / 下图
Blessed Vault of West Qing Mausoleum (Mu Mausoleum) / Lower

神树与大清的命运

站在宝顶前，最先看见的就是宝顶上的那棵神树，这就是传说中与大清命运息息相关的昭陵神树。在墓前种树，可追溯到秦朝，在孔子去世后形成风气。而清朝在宝顶上种榆树的原因，不仅是受汉文化影响，还有一个重要的原因，就是榆树与爱新觉罗氏先祖，有一段传奇的渊源。

最早在宝顶种树的是永陵，福陵和昭陵都为附会永陵，在宝顶种了榆树。然而与昭陵、福陵不同的是，永陵神榆，并不是种在宝顶上，而是种在五个宝顶中间最大的衣冠冢前，两侧四个宝顶呈"U"形排列，将神榆围在中间。关于永陵主顶上的榆树，民间有很多传说。传说当年那棵树上附有"悬龙"，恰巧被努尔哈赤的先祖压住，因而才有了后来的大清基业。而神树的命运，也似乎真的与大清的命运有关。1863年，永陵枝繁叶茂的"神树"被大风吹倒，巨大的树枝将永陵启运殿的屋顶都压坏了。同治皇帝感到此事不吉利，命两位大臣赶往东北，用木墩子撑住神树。然而，所有努力都无济于事，神树最终还是连根烂掉了。此时的清朝，已经开始衰落。

永陵神树，在清朝末年也出现了问题，据传溥仪还特意请来日本专家给神树看病，至今在昭陵神树前还留有当年为了支撑即将倒伏的神树而立铜杆的水泥座。而不管溥仪请人给神树看病是真是假，但是大清的命运最终真的完结了。昭陵宝顶在"文化大革命"时倒塌了，经过修缮，尽管福陵没有宝顶塌陷，神树也没有受到损坏，但是昭陵神树，是目前"关外三陵"中长势最好最茂盛的。

DIVINE TREE AND FATE OF GREAT QING DYNASTY

Standing in front of Blessed Vault of the Mausoleum, you will first catch sight of the elm on the Vault, which is called Divine Tree in the legend. The Tree is said to have close relationship with the fate of Qing Dynasty. The practice of planting trees in front of mausoleums can be traced back to Qin Dynasty, and it is widely accepted since Confucius' death. Planting elms on top of the mounds in Qing Dynasty was not only due to the influences of Han culture, but also due to the legendary relationship between the elm and Aisin Gioro's ancestors.

Yong Mausoleum's Vault was the first to be planted with an elm, followed by Fu Mausoleum and Zhaoling Imperial Tomb. Divine Trees of Zhaoling Imperial Tomb and Fu Mausoleum are planted on the vaults, but in contrast, the elm of Yong Mausoleum is planted not on Blessed Vault but in front of the biggest cenotaph. The other four vaults surround the elm in a U-shape. It is said that there was a "suspended dragon" on the elm, which happened to be suppressed by Nurhaci's ancestors. Then there came prosperity of Qing Dynasty. The fate of Divine Tree seemed to have some connections with that of Qing Dynasty indeed. In 1863, Divine Tree of Yong Mausoleum with luxuriant foliage was blown down by a windstorm. and its huge branches broke the roof of Luck-provoking Hall. Emperor Tongzhi felt uneasy about this event, so he ordered two chancellors to prop up Divine Tree with a block of wood. All their efforts turned out to be in vain, and at last even roots of the Tree were rotten. From that time on, Qing Dynasty began to decline.

Divine Tree of Yong Mausoleum also became ill at the end of Qing Dynasty. It is said that Pu Yi had invited experts from Japan to check it. Today we can still see the cement column used to hold the copper pole supporting the lodging tree. Regardless the validity of the story, the reign of Qing came to an end. The Vault of Zhaoling Imperial Tomb collapsed during the Cultural Revolution, and it was later renovated. Although the Vault of Fu Mausoleum wa not collapsed, and its Divine Tree was not damaged. Divine Tree of Zhaoling Imperial Tomb is currently the most luxurious in Three Mausoleums of Shengjing.

西照宝顶 / 左图
Blessed Vault in Sunset / Left
雪罩宝顶 / 右页图
Blessed Vault in Snow / Right Page

宝顶的秘密

顺着月牙城两侧的蹬道继续走便到了宝城，这是一座半圆形的城，城高7.84米，周长201.3米。宝城中间有个丘冢，就是宝顶，这宝顶是用三合土（白灰、砂子和黄土）夯筑而成，每当太阳西斜，阳光照射在宝顶之上，这宝顶便有如同一面斜放的"镜子"，熠熠发光，充分昭示了皇家应有的霸气，也成为著名的"昭陵十景"（注解14）之一。关外三陵比较，永陵宝顶在山坡底下，在启运山脚下，且数量达五个之多。而昭陵、福陵都只有一个宝顶，而昭陵宝顶建在平原上，福陵宝顶则在山上。

宝顶之下便是地宫——整个陵寝的心脏部位，自古以来，由于葬有皇帝和皇后，地宫便是一个讳莫如深的地方，各种史书都对地宫缄口不言，生怕言词闪失之间有辱皇体，招来横祸。然而欲盖弥彰，地宫也往往会成为一个众说纷纭的神秘之处。

地宫附近中有很多森森古树，让人一靠近便心中凛然，这些参天古树围绕着地宫，好像把它包围在自己的怀抱中，尽心守护。至今为止，昭陵地宫从未开启，不过从明十三陵及清乾隆、慈禧等陵寝的结构，可以大致推测出昭陵地宫的结构。地宫内部，一般四壁都刻有精美的壁画，有随葬品，并有几层厚重的石门，每层门用"自来石"封闭。宝顶之下，究竟埋藏着多少秘密，已成为世界之谜。

SECRETS OF BLESSED VAULT

Following the way of Crescent City, you will see Blessed Bastion, which is 7.84 meters high and 201.3 meters in perimeter. The Vault is right in its middle, armored with triple-combined soil (lime, sand and loess). Every day when the sun sets, the sunlight shines over the Vault which resembles like a tilted mirror, shining with radiance and fully exposing its supremacy, thus becoming one of the famous "Ten Scenic Spots of Zhaoling Imperial Tomb" (see Note 14). Among the three Qing emperor mausoleums outside Shanhai Pass, there are five vaults inside Yong Mausoleum, and they are all at the foot of Qiyun Mount (Luck-provoking Mount), but there is only one in Zhaoling Imperial Tomb and Fu Mausoleum, and the Vault of Zhaoling Imperial Tomb is built on flat plain while that of Fu Mausoleumis on a hill.

Under the Vault is the underground palace – the central part of the Mausoleum. From the ancient time, the underground palace is a secret closely guarded since it is the final resting habitat for the remains of emperor and empress. All historical records skipped it over afraid of insulting the imperial system and incurring disasters. However, the more one tries to hide, the more curious others will beome, and so the underground palace was in fact a frequently talked mysterious place.

Awe-inspiring dense trees grow near the underground palace, and fear will clinch your heart once you step closer. These tall trees surround the underground palace, embracing it as devoted guards. Till now, the underground palace of Zhaoling Imperial Tomb has never been opened. However, from Ming Thirteen Tombs and mausoleums of Emperor Qianlong and Empress Dowager Cixi, we can roughly infer the inner structure of Zhaoling Imperial Tomb. Inside the underground palace, it has four walls inscribed with murals, sacrificial objects, and a couple of heavy stone gates, each covered with "auto-sliding stone" (used to protect the tomb). Secrets under theVault remain unearthed, and become worldwide puzzles.

古松也是文物

现在的昭陵，作为公园，里面种了很多新植物，里面树木繁多，生态环境很好，漫步其间，经常能看见可爱的小松鼠在前面蹦蹦跳跳。昭陵的一大特色就是漫漫数里的古松群，昭陵里现存古松两千余棵，松龄都达三百多年，摇曳挺拔，参天蔽日，这些古松和建筑一起长存在这片土地上，也是文物，是陵寝重要的组成部分。在清朝时，这些古松的栽植是十分讲究的，根据《大清宝典》中记载，陵区松树其实有"山树"、"仪树"、"海树"、"荡树"之分。"山树"栽在隆业山周围，"海树"栽植在风水红墙以外，"仪树"是指分列在隆恩门前神道两旁的八棵树，也称"站班树"和"八大朝臣"；"荡树"是指风水红墙里的树，其排列有序，十分整齐。此外，对栽种后松树的管理也十分严格，对树木逐一建立档案记载，凡枯死、倒伏、砍伐者一律上报盛京将军批准后才能处理。不准多种，也不准少种，遵循死一棵补种一棵的原则。如今，作为公园，这些苍翠的陵松在金瓦红墙中构成昭陵一道壮丽景观，人们根据古树的形状纷纷给树起了很多有趣的名字，比如"凤凰树"、"夫妻树"、"姐妹树"、"龟树"等，并演绎了很多传说。而这些传说中，最著名的就是关于宝顶"神树"的，尤其是神树与大清的命运息息相关的传说，更被人津津乐道。不过比较遗憾的是，现在的很多人并不了解古代的种树制度，在陵区里种植了大量的新树，使陵区的古松显得杂乱，而失去了以往的威严阵势。

观音柏 / 下图
Buddha Cypress / Lower
陵寝后的古松 / 右页图
Aged Pine Tree behind the Mausoleum / Right Page

AGED PINES ARE ALSO ANTIQUITY

A variety of new arbores have been planted inside Zhaoling Imperial Tomb because it is a park now. Due to its exuberant trees and excellent ecological environment, lovely squirrels often emerge and hop off in the woods. Visitors may notice a distinctive feature of Zhaoling Imperial Tomb - stretching of aged pine trees. There exists more than two thousand pine trees inside the Mausoleum, and they are over three hundred years old. These towering pine trees are tall, straight, and really impressive. In Qing Dynasty, planting of these pines were under strict control. According to records of Collection of Great Qing, pines of Zhaoling Imperial Tomb fall into four kinds as "hill tree," "posture tree," "sea tree," and "swing tree." Hill trees are planted around Longye hill while sea trees outside the geomantic red walls; posture trees refer to the 8 pines on both sides of Spirit Path in front of Eminent Favor Gate, also known as "standing trees" and "Eight courtiers," while swing trees refer to the trees in neat sequence inside the geomantic red walls. In addition, management of planted pine trees is also very strict: files for every pine will be created, and all the dead, lodging, chopped down trees must be submitted to General of Shengjing for approval. The principle is strictly followed that no more or no less trees can be planted and only one pine can be planted when one died. Now these verdant pine trees display in the park a splendid view with the setting of golden glazed tiles and red wall. And people name these trees according to their appearances, such as Phoenix Pine, Couple Pine, Sister Pine and Turtle Pine, from which, of course, many interesting folklores originate. One of the most well-known is about Divine Tree of Blessed Vault, which is frequently said to be closely connected with the fate of Qing Dynasty. Unfortunately, many people know nothing about ancient arbor system and plant many new trees inside the Mausoleum, depriving the ancient pines of its magnificent air.

哪来的蛇神庙

在昭陵内,更衣亭后身儿,风水红墙外有一个坐北朝南的方形小庙,原来的蛇神庙门楣石门额上有一种奇特的文体写着"蛇神庙",笔画弯曲,如蜿蜒爬行的蛇一样,我想这可能就是"鸟篆"。而如今蛇神庙经过现代修缮,门上的匾额已是规矩的金色楷体字,令人遗憾。蛇神庙隐藏在树林里,小时候去昭陵因为害怕我从没走近过。一直到我在昭陵寻找御厕排水处时从后面看到它,那时起它才从我小时候的阴影里走出来,走进我的视线。拍摄时,因为想到蛇,我刻意放大了树枝印在地上的光影,明暗交错之间,仿佛蛇行。庙前有两个石狮子,让人一直心存疑问,它们的背面是平的,显然应是靠在什么建筑上的,而不属于这里。对于这个小庙来说,这两只狮子也未免太大了。它们从何而来,应在何处?似乎已经不可考。

我在清代其他皇陵没见过蛇神庙,可以说这是昭陵独有的。关于这个小庙的传说,丰富多彩。有人说,这里供奉着一条叫"金花教主"的巨蟒,因为它救过皇太极的命,皇太极称帝后就命人修建了这座庙。不过传说真的只能是听听故事而已,经不起推敲,皇太极时根本没有建自己的陵寝,"皮之不存毛将焉附"?昭陵都没有建,这个蛇神小庙又怎么能存在呢?而另外一个传说,则跟小庙的重建有关。相传,一年夏天,张学良与赵四小姐来昭陵别墅避暑。当晚,赵四小姐梦见一条红蛇,口吐人言。赵四把梦讲给张学良,张学良不信,赵四忙说:"那蛇说,如能给它找个住所,帮你报杀父之仇。"张学良报仇心切,于是出资重修了这庙。而也有史料记载,说这庙是奉天省长莫德惠重修的。我觉得小庙出现在民国时期的这个时间倒是可信的,赵四做梦一说,杜撰的可能性大些,事实究竟如何,还是留给后人去考证吧。

至于皇陵里出现蛇神庙,民间传说,蛇是龙的化身,因此,蛇也被称为可以守护陵寝的"灵"。我在研究中国广告史的时候,也论证过蛇的演变过程,作为整个中华民族的图腾,龙,其实也有蛇的组成部分。现在在民间,甚至还有将蛇叫作"小龙"的说法。而皇帝自视为真龙天子,对蛇当然也会另眼相看。此外,古时我国北方一些民族崇拜萨满教,信奉万物有灵论。在关于满族先人的英雄传说《东海窝集传》中记载了:"满族人对蛇和熊既尊重又讨厌。……看到蛇就急忙跪下磕头,因为蛇太多,无法磕拜。"这说明,古代的满族是崇拜蛇的。在汉族人来讲,女娲伏羲都是蛇的化身,清代皇帝多讲究融合汉文化,对蛇的理解受到了汉文化的影响也是有可能的。

MYSTERIES OF ZOMBIE TEMPLE

At the back of Dressing House inside Zhaoling Imperial Tomb, there is a small square temple facing south near the geomantic red wall. The stone board on top of the temple's gate used to be engraved with characters in a strange style "Zombie Temple," which feels like a wriggling snake likely to be bird script (an ancient form of Chinese written characters, resembling birds' footprints). Zombie Temple is hidden among the woods, and I had never plucked up my courage to approach it when I was young because of fear. I couldn't walk out of the fearful shadow of Zombie Temple until one time I set eyes on it when I was searching for the drainage system of Imperial Toilet. I purposely zoomed in for the shadow of tree branches on the ground when I took a photo of Zombie Temple, as the shadow resembled really crawling snakes. There are two stone lions in front of the temple, which incurred my suspicion. Obviously they are not located here properly, for their backs are flat and even, and they are larger for such a small temple. However, it remains a mystery and seems unsolvable from where they are moved and where they should be located.

I have never found traces of zombie temples in other imperial mausoleums of Qing Dynasty, and the one in Zhaoling Imperial Tomb is unique. There are many colorful myths regarding this temple. According to folklore, a giant boa named "Golden Flower Hierarch" was worshiped in this temple, for it had once saved the life of Hong Taiji. The temple was erected here under the order of Hong Taiji after he proclaimed himself emperor. But such kind of tales

should not be treated seriously, for there were no sound proofs. Zhaoling Imperial Tomb was still not built when Hong Taiji was alive. So how could the building of Zombie Temple be possible when the Mausoleum itself didn't exist? Yet there is another legend about rebuilding this temple. It is said that one summer Zhang Xueliang and Miss Zhao Si came to Zhaoling Imperial Tomb Villa for holidays. At night, Miss Zhao Si dreamt of a red snake talking to her. Afterwards, Miss Zhao told her dream to Zhang Xueliang, who didn't believe it at first. Then Miss Zhao promptly said, "That snake told me she would avenge your father's death if you could build a shelter for her." Zhang was eager to take revenge at that time, and so he spent money and renovated the temple. But as in some historical records, the temple was rebuilt by Mo Dehui, Governor of Mukden. But personally I favor the version that the temple was built in the period of Republic of China, and the dream of Miss Zhao is more likely to be fabricated. But now the riddle regarding the building of Zombie Temple is still there, waiting to be solved and verified by later generation.

From the perspective of folklore belief of China, snake is regarded as reincarnation of dragon, and therefore, snake can be deemed as the guarding spirit of mausoleum. When I was studying advertising history of China, I expounded on the symbolic evolution of snake. Dragon is symbol and totem of China as a nation, and it takes on some features of a snake. So some people in some regions of China still name the snake "dragonet." Emperors were looked upon as "the true dragon and real son of Heaven," and snakes were also treated with special respect. Besides, some northern races of ancient China worshiped shamanism, believing in animism. A book describing the epic adventures of Manchu ancestors records, "Manchu people both admire and hate snakes and bears ... they make a kowtow to a snake at the sight of it." The recording proves that Manchu admired snakes in ancient time. From the viewpoint of Han nationality, Nü Wa (Goddess of Sky-patching) and Fu Xi (Fu His, God of Fishery and Husbandry) are both thought to be embodiments of snake. Emperors of Qing Dynasty attached importance to combination of Han culture with Manchu culture, and their understanding of snake was likely to be influenced by Han culture.

陵园内的松鼠／左页图
Squirrel inside the Mausoleum / Left Page
蛇神庙／上图
Zombie Temple / Upper
［全高3米，长、宽各2.63米］
(3 meters tall, 2.63 meters long and wide)

结语
——四十三年分之一秒

四十三是我现在的年纪,一秒是我记录下昭陵的一瞬间所用的时间。这两个看似不相干的数字,就在我的生命中,有了一次次美妙的融合。画册中的每一幅照片都占据着我四十三年的生命长度,落定画笔或是按住快门的一秒钟。在别人看来它也许是再简单不过的一个画面,但对于我而言,却是值得我无限回味的"赵琛时间"的一秒钟。

从开始学习画画,我就常常一个人来昭陵写生,那里的一草一木可以说都是我绘画上的启蒙老师,激发着我对"观察"这件事的热爱,也无声地指导着我对事物的认识。后来,我有了自己的相机,我就常常一个人去那里照相,从胶片到数码,如果用数字来计算的话,我想我是无论如何也给不出精确数字的,的确太庞大了。春去冬来春又回,就这样在平常不过的日子里,四十三年原来也匆匆。

四十三年来,积累下的和昭陵有关的作品,根本无从计数。如果把这些一个又一个一秒连在一起,不知道又占据了我多少光景。这是一笔财富,任再凶悍的强盗也奈他不何,因为它已经融入我生命的每一个晨曦黄昏;这是人生履历上对我生命的另一番呈现,任再无情的岁月也奈他不何,因为它已经见证了我生命的每一次成长浮沉。

积累和沉淀,对于艺术都是莫大的考验。一个地方再美,也不是一天甚至几年就可以记录完的,有的时候我在昭陵拍一天,都拍不出一张满意的作品。而一秒而成的作品又是天赐,多少美丽的时刻别人没有遇到,却恰恰被我碰到了。宝顶上的那株神树,在它最精彩的时候被我捕捉到了,等我再去时,它已经因雷击而死了,那一刻我是那么庆幸我记录它的那一秒钟,很多东西没了就真的没了。我想这是我和昭陵言说不出的缘分吧。

正是有了这时间的跨度和我与昭陵多年培养出的莫名默契,有了照片十几年的沉淀,我才开始有胆量表现这件人类杰出的艺术品。做这本画册的初衷是,我想昭陵最美的瞬间能让更多的人看到,而最不容易的地方也恰恰就在这儿。什么才是最美的昭陵?选片的时候这个问题常常难倒我自己。即使是一张照片,我也是隔了很久再看看,看看是不是还是觉得一样精彩。这些昭陵的画或是照片,真的成了我多少年来良苦用心的心血。

作品是一种人生体悟的表达,同样的地点,同样的时间,甚至同一个位置同一个角度,照出来的昭陵都不一样。什么变了?昭陵沉淀的历史更厚重了,它在变,但更重要的是看风景的人也在变。四十几年,心境变了,感受多了,阅历深了,同样的景物有了不同的领悟,自然也就照出了不同的感觉。透过这么多年的作品,我在一个个一秒钟中,回味着自己的经历,恍惚间竟也模糊地看出了四十三年来成长的影子。纵使在昭陵拍摄已经有二十余年了,但是我仍然

17岁画石牌坊(1984年) / Stone Memorial arch Drawn at the Age of 17 (1984)

没有拍全传说中的"昭陵十景",只是这些年的工作,不是我一个人努力的结果,没有沈阳市城市建设管理局对我的全力支持,没有昭陵全体工作人员的配合,我也不可能完成这一秒一秒的工作,即使有了这一秒的时间,如果没有适合的天气和光线,我同样不能完成这一秒的工作,可以说这一秒是"天时地利人和"同时具备才能完成的。为此,我内心充满了感激。

四十三年,生死的事情自然看得多了。随着这些年游历四方的经历,看多了陵寝,也自然而然的,对生与死、对皇陵有了更深刻的理解。生是偶然,逝是必然。

世界万物都有起点和终点,人也是一样,一辈子是一场生的跋涉,同时也是一场死的奔赴,我们从来都无法选择自己什么时候出生,在哪出生,因此落地之时,婴孩都是无奈的哭着的。而当一个人在世上走了几十载之后,他又不可逃脱的归于死亡。人始于生,而归于死,生的跋涉是为了更好地赴死,古人在这一点上却比我们很多现代人都看得明白。古代皇帝在世之时就开始为自己修葺墓地园陵,便是因为他们深知死的必然,因而早早地为自己的"死"做好打算。

帝王作为一个时代的领导者,投身于帝王之家,是一种有幸,可以锦衣玉食,受万人敬仰;亦是一种不幸,他们一开始就无从选择自己的命运,正如南唐后主李煜,或许生做一个落魄的书生更适合他的品性,历史上会少了一个被

15岁画昭陵秋天景色(1982年) / Autumn of Zhaoling Imperial Tomb at the Age of 15(1982)

幽禁的君主,而多了一个更富才情的词人。生命伴随着这种偶然而来的,要背负着生的责任,坚定地走下去。于是帝王便将对于生命的唯一一点操纵权留在了"逝"上,"纵使千年铁门槛,终须一个土馒头。"再多的繁华也会落地成泥,回归虚空之境,死后灵魂的安宁抑或是延续生前的辉煌,都寄托在了死后的事情上。也就因此,中国有了隆重的死后祭祀和礼仪,有了巍巍皇陵的气派,成就了中华的磅礴大气、向死而生的陵寝建筑风格,形成了中国顶级的丧葬文化。在清昭陵中,这些思想都可以很强烈地感受得到。

大丈夫,生何忧,死何惧?学地质的人有这样一种说法,如果把地球的存在说成是一小时的话,那整个人类的生命就是两秒。现在的人们感受的时间长度都是人为赋予的,人类为了生存的方便自己给自己定了时间,对于浩渺的苍穹来说,它只是自顾自地晨昏交替,有着自己的章法。人类的生命都如此短暂,更何况人的短短数十载呢?那人就更没有什么可畏惧的了。在我以秒为计量单位的生命中,我用四十三年分之一秒记录了我眼中昭陵的一瞬……

到此书出版的时候,我对书中的图片、文字、版式等都不是很满意,研究昭陵的工作不是我人生的全部,实在缺少时间,只能仓促交稿,定有缺憾,留后世评说吧!

公元二〇〇九年春
于九平书屋

CONCLUSION
—1 SECOND V.S. 43 YEARS

43 is my current age, and 1 second refers to that flash of time I use to take photos of Zhaoling Imperial Tomb. The two seeming irrelevant numbers, however, are amazingly integrated in my life. Each picture in the photo album takes an elapsed second of my lifetime for sketches or snapshots. In the eyes of others, it is only a simple picture, but as for me it's an indispensable "My Time" that I would recall thousands of times.

When I began to learn drawing, I liked to frequent Zhaoling Imperial Tomb for sketches. Every blade of grass and every tree there inspired my drawings, stimulating my observation and directing my perception over things. Later when I had my own camera, I often visited Zhaoling Imperial Tomb and took photos, first with a film camera, later a digital one. Statistically, I have no way to give an exact number of how many photos I have taken, which is too colossal. Springs and winters give way to each other alternatively. In such a simple manner, 43 years of my life passed in a rush.

During the 43 years, I took countless photos of Zhaoling Imperial Tomb. If these photos were spliced together, nobody knows how many more seconds it would take me, for there are too many of them. They are my wealth and there is no way to deprive them of my heart, even for the most ferocious robber. They have been integrated into each dawn and dusk of my life. They embody my life and thus witness the ups and downs of my growth, together with the relentless lapse of time.

Accumulation and sedimentation are both utmost tests to art. No matter how beautiful a place is, it takes more than one day or a couple of years to record. Sometimes I spent an entire day in Zhaoling Imperial Tomb to take an ideal photo, but still failed. One time, I snapped the most brilliant moment of Divine Tree on the Blessed Vault in my photo, however, when I came again, it had already died of the lightning's strike. While remorse lingers in my heart for its loss, I, on the other hand, felt lucky to be able to catch that moment. A lot of things are gone just in a flash, but many memorable aspects of Zhaoling Imperial Tomb are kept among my photos, which might present my inexplicable pre-destined relation with Zhaoling Imperial Tomb.

17岁画昭陵石牌坊（1984年冬）

Stone Paifang of Zhaoling Imperial Tomb Drawn at the Age of 17 (in the winter of 1984)

Backed by my long-cherished love and obsession toward Zhaoling Imperial Tomb as well as photos taken over the past years, I venture to show to others magnificence of Zhaoling Imperial Tomb through this book. My intention is to let more people to enjoy the most beautiful moments of Zhaoling Imperial Tomb, and it is also a really tough job to select suitable photos as illustrations. I always watch these photos again and again before making my final decisions, for they are all fabulous products of my painstaking efforts.

Works are expressions of one's life experience. Photos are different even though they are taken at the same time and place, from the same perspective and angle, for Zhaoling Imperial Tomb has changed over the time. After over forty years' life, I have also changed, thus always having a different understanding over the same scene. Through these works and from each photo I took, I can recollect my past and find my growing traces. Although I have been shooting pictures of Zhaoling Imperial Tomb for more than twenty years, I am still not able to shoot all the legendary "Zhaoling Imperial Tomb Ten Sceneries." However, all the works of these years were not completed all by myself: I could not finish all these works without full support of Shenyang Urban Construction Authority and cooperation of all the staff in Fu Mausoleum; I still could not do this one-second job if the weather and light are not appropriate even if I have time. It can be said that this one-second requires "good timing, geographical convenience and good human relations." Accordingly, I am much filled with gratitude.

For 43 years, I have experienced and savored many ups and downs in life, including life and death. With rich travel experiences around the world and frequent visits to mausoleums, I have gained a deep understanding about imperial mausoleums as well as to life itself. Birth brings new life while death cannot be avoided.

Everything in the universe has its start and ending, and the same is true for human beings. One's lifetime is more or less like a trudge and a march to death. We can never choose when and where to begin our life. That is why babies cry when they are born for their powerlessness in choosing their starting point. However, people fight during our lifetime to live and achieve though no one is immortal. The ancient people were more open-minded regarding death than we are. The emperors started building their own tombs during their lifetime as they know they were going to die one day, and it was always sane to make preparation at an earlier time.

Emperors were fortunate, on one hand, as they were born into their royal family and lived extravagant lives, and they could reign a country for a particular period and be venerated by their subjects. On the other hand, they were unlucky considering that they couldn't decide their own fates, which were predestined from their birth. Take Last Emperor of Southern Tang, Li Yi, for

18岁画昭陵晚秋（1985年10月6日）
Late Autumn of Zhaoling Imperial Tomb Drawn at the Age of 18 (in October 6, 1985)

昭陵在辽宁省沈阳市的位置／上图
Location of Zhaoling Imperial Tomb in Shenyang, Liaoning Province / Upper
辽宁省沈阳市在中国的位置／下图
Location of Shenyang, Liaoning Province in China / Lower
昭陵平面图／右页图
Zhaoling Imperial Tomb Plan / Right Page

example, it was more suitable for him to be born as an intellectual rather than an emperor. In that case, he would not have been under house arrest and could become a brilliant poet. Emperors had to take the obligations and stepped down the road unhesitatingly, although some of them might prefer different lives. Their only freedom was to decide the way they were buried. "Emperors and great people may live splendid and adventurous lives, but what they need is only an earthen mound to bury their bodies finally." A bustling life would finally end, so the emperors had to seek their tranquility of soul or their extension of a glorious life from their tombs and hence ways of offering sacrifice after their later lives. It is right based on these considerations, China formed grand sacrifice ceremonies and rituals, built many magnificent imperial mausoleums with majestic architectural style, and formed an incomparable funeral culture. Zhaoling Imperial Tomb is in fact of a perfect example of this funeral culture.

A true man never shows worries and fear of death during his lifetime. Those who specialize in geology would like to describe existence of the Earth within "one hour." In that case, existence of human beings is about two seconds. The present perceptions of time are all set by human beings for convenience of living. But actually, individual life is as short as a flash. Life of human beings is so transient and short, so we don't even have the time to be fearful of its elapsing. So it brings pleasure and satisfaction to devote my time to recording Zhaoling Imperial Tomb in the snaps of lens …

Till publication of this book, I am still not much satisfied with these pictures, texts and layout. The research on Zhaoling Imperial Tomb is not my whole life, and I can do nothing but deliver these pictures and writings in haste, due to lack of time. The book will for sure have its regrettable shortcomings, however, criticism from readers are all welcome.

At Jiuping Study, in the Spring of 2009

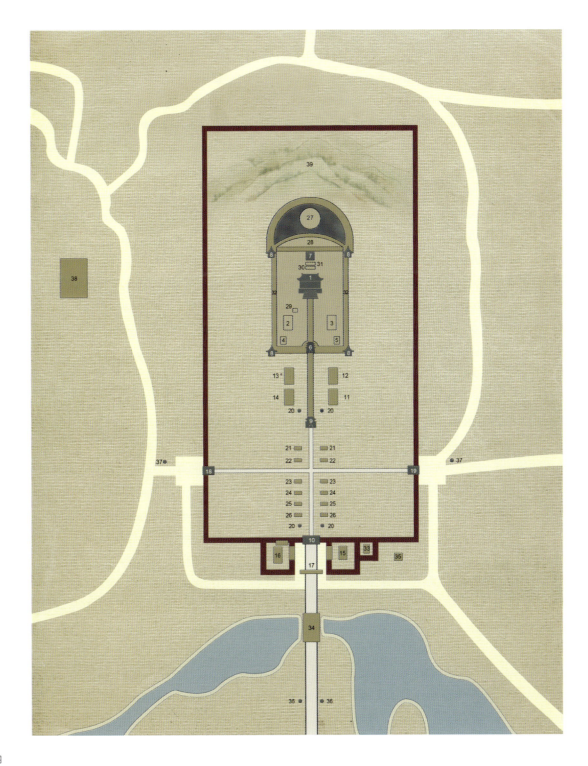

昭陵平面图
Ichnography of Zhaoling Imperial Tomb

1.	隆恩殿	Eminent Favor Hall	14.	果房	Fruit House	28.	月牙城	Crescent City
2.	西配殿	West Side-hall	15.	更衣房	Dressing House	29.	焚帛亭	Silk-burning Pavilion
3.	东配殿	East Side-hall	16.	宰牲厅	Animal Killing House	30.	二柱门	Dual Pillar Gate
4.	西晾果楼	West Fruit Airing House	17.	石牌坊	Stone Paifang	31.	石五供	Stone Five Offerings
5.	东晾果楼	East Fruit Airing House	18.	西红门	West Red Gate	32.	方城马道	Horse Track of Square City
6.	隆恩门、五凤楼	Eminent Favor Gate, Five Phoenix Tower	19.	东红门	East Red Gate	33.	御厕	Imperial Toilet
7.	大明楼	Grand Ming Tower	20.	华表	Huabiao	34.	神桥	Spirit Bridge
8.	角楼	Turret	21.	石象生（立象）	Stone Elephant Statue	35.	蛇神庙	Zombie Temple
9.	碑楼	Stele Pavilion	22.	石象生（骆驼）	Stone Camel Statue	36.	石狮	Stone Lion
10.	正红门	Front Red Gate	23.	石象生（立马）	Stone Horse Statue	37.	下马碑	Dismounting Tablet
11.	涤器房	Cleaning House	24.	石象生（麒麟）	Stone Kylin Statue	38.	贵妃园寝遗址	Relic of Burial Garden for Noble Concubines
12.	茶膳房	Tea and Food House	25.	石象生（獬豸）	Stone Xie Zhi Statue			
13.	仪仗房	Honor Guards House	26.	石象生（狮子）	Stone Lion Statue	39.	隆业山	Hill Longye
			27.	宝顶	Blessed Vault, Blessed Mound			

注解

注解 1：太湖三白，中国第二大淡水湖太湖名食，以太湖银鱼、白鱼、白虾三味湖鲜之形冠名。

注解 2：智者乐水，语出《论语·雍也》"知者乐水，仁者乐山；知者动，仁者静；知者乐，仁者寿"。知，同智。知者，达于事理而周流无滞，有似于水，故乐水。仁者，安于义理而厚重不迁，有似于山，故乐山。也有将"五行"之说引入者，云："知者属土，故乐水；仁者属木，故乐山。"关于三个乐字的读音，也一直存在争议。可以明确的是前两个乐字音相同，有说音 yao，也有说音 yue 的属于通假字，第三乐字则取本意，音也为现代的 le。

注解 3：黄帝陵：是中华民族始祖黄帝轩辕氏的陵寝，相传黄帝得道升天，故此陵寝为衣冠冢。位于陕西黄陵县城北桥山；1961 年，国务院公布为全国第一批全国重点文物保护单位，编为"古墓葬第一号"，号称"天下第一陵"。

炎帝陵：炎帝陵一共有三个，分别是"湖南省炎陵县炎帝陵"、"陕西省宝鸡市炎帝陵"和"山西省高平市炎帝陵"。

大禹陵：大禹陵位于绍兴稽山门外，距城 3 公里。大禹陵本身是一座规模宏大的古典风格建筑群，由禹陵、禹祠、禹庙三部分组成，占地 40 余亩，建筑面积 2700 多平方米，被列为全国重点文物保护单位。

少昊陵：黄帝之子少昊建都穷桑，后徙曲阜，在位 84 年，寿百岁而终，葬于鲁故城东门之外的寿丘，位于曲阜城东 4 公里的旧县村东北，陵阔 28.5 米，高 8.73 米，顶立 12 米，形如金字塔，有"中国金字塔"之称。

秦始皇陵：秦始皇陵位于距西安市 30 多公里的临潼县城以东的骊山脚下。史书记载：秦始皇嬴政从 13 岁即位时就开始营建陵园，由丞相李斯主持规划设计，大将章邯监工，修筑时间长达 38 年，工程之浩大、气魄之宏伟，创历代封建统治者奢侈厚葬之先例。

汉武帝陵：汉武帝刘彻是历史上可以和秦始皇相提并论的很有才略的封建帝王，他的陵寝茂陵位于西安市西北 40 公里的兴平市（原兴平县）城东北南位乡茂陵村。公元前 139 年至前 87 年间建成，历时 53 年，现为全国重点文物保护单位。

光武帝陵：东汉光武帝刘秀（前 6—后 57 年）字文叔，南阳蔡阳〔今湖北枣阳西南人〕高祖九世孙。光武帝陵，亦称刘秀坟，在河南孟津县铁谢村附近。南依邙山，北濒黄河。陵寝为高大的土冢，周围 1400 米，高 20 米，古柏千余株，苍劲挺拔，阴郁幽静。

唐太宗陵：唐太宗李世民是唐朝第二代皇帝，他的陵寝与清朝开国皇帝皇太极的陵寝有着相同的名字，同为昭陵，唐昭陵是陕西关中"唐十八陵"中规模最大的一座，位于陕西省礼泉县城东北 22.5 公里的九嵕山上。

唐高宗与武则天陵：武则天是中国历史上唯一的女皇帝，同时也是继位年龄最大（67 岁即位），寿命最长的皇帝之一（终年 82 岁）。唐高宗时为皇后、唐中宗和唐睿宗时为皇太后，后自立为武周皇帝，改"唐"为"周"，定都洛阳，史称"武周"或"南周"，705 年退位，死后要求与唐高宗李治合葬。陵寝位于西安乾县。乾陵，是中国乃至世界上独一无二的一座两朝帝王、一对夫妻皇帝合葬陵。建于 684 年，历时 23 年才修建完成。

宋太祖赵匡胤陵：赵匡胤（927-976 年），涿州（今河北省涿县）人。他曾是后周王朝的殿前都点检，领宋州归德军节度使，执掌军权。960 年，他发动"陈桥兵变"，即位，称国号"宋"，建立了宋王朝，定都河南开封。宋太祖死于 976 年，葬于巩义市宋陵陵区，陵名永昌。

宋神宗赵顼陵：赵顼自幼"好学请问，至日晏忘食"。当太子时就喜读《韩非子》，1067-1085 年在位。死后葬于永裕陵，1085 年建造，该陵石刻是宋陵晚期造像的代表，陵中石狮的造型和雕工，在宋陵诸石刻中，位列榜首。人们品评宋陵石雕说："东陵狮子，西陵象，滹沱河上好石羊"。

宋哲宗赵煦陵：宋哲宗赵煦（1076 - 1100 年），北宋第七位皇帝，宋神宗第六子，原名佣，曾被封为延安郡王。永泰陵位于巩县芝田乡八陵村村南，东北距芝田镇八华里，东南距永裕陵约 400 米。永泰陵遭到金朝的多次破坏，最残忍的一次，宋哲宗的尸骨也被露掷在永泰陵外，后为臣子包裹重新放置陵中，今日的永泰陵也只剩下一个光秃秃的土丘了。

成吉思汗陵：成吉思汗陵在内蒙古鄂尔多斯市伊金霍洛旗甘德利草原上，距东胜区 70 公里。蒙古族盛行"密葬"，所以真正的成吉思汗陵究竟在何处始终是个谜。现今的成吉思汗陵是一座衣冠冢，它经过多次迁移，直到 1954 年才由湟中县的塔尔寺迁回故地伊金霍洛旗，北距包头市 185 公里。

明孝陵：明孝陵在南京市东郊紫金山（钟山）南麓独龙阜玩珠峰下，茅山西侧。明朝开国皇帝朱元璋和皇后马氏合葬于此。明孝陵是现存建筑规模最大的古代帝王陵寝之一，其陵寝制度既继承了唐宋及之前帝陵"依山为陵"的制度，又通过改方坟为圆丘，开创了陵寝建筑"前方后圆"的基本格局。

明十三陵：明朝皇帝的墓葬群，因葬有十三位皇帝而得名。在北京西北郊昌平区境内的燕山山麓的天寿山。自永乐七年（1409 年）五月始作长陵，到明朝最后一帝崇祯葬入思陵止，230 多年间，先后修建了十三座皇帝陵寝、七座妃子墓、一座太监墓。共埋葬了十三位皇帝、二十三位皇后、二位太子、三十余名妃嫔、一位太监。

注解 4：天葬，在我国，天葬是西藏地方古老而独特的风俗习惯，也是大部分西藏人采用的丧葬方法，亦称"鸟葬"。天葬有固定的天葬场，人死后，由专门的背尸人将尸体背到天葬场，然后天葬师把尸体背朝着天，折断四肢，在尸体中央和两肩用力撕开皮肤露出肌肉，然后退开，苍鹰铺天盖地而下竞争啄食。天葬台上剩下骷髅时天葬师用石头将骷髅敲成骨酱揉成一团，秃鹫再次铺天盖地而下，食尽散去，周围的人开始长跪顶礼。天葬作为丧葬仪式之一，本质上是一种社会文化现象。

注解 5：兄弟民族，作者观点，被汉化程度较高的，在体貌特征，生活习性上与汉族接近的都是兄弟民族。

注解 6：昭陵选址者，一直是个谜，没有明确记载，在康熙四年三月，"荣亲王园寝选址案"中，得知杜如预、杨宏量二人被免死的原因，是康熙念其二人曾为永陵、福陵、昭陵选址有功。

注解 7：此句出自出处《孟子·尽心下》，其意为贤人先使自己明白，然后才去使别人明白；今天的人则是自己都没有搞清楚，却想去使别人明白。

注解 8：牌楼，起源于棂星门，开始用于祭天、祀孔，滥觞于汉阙，成熟于唐、宋，至明、清登峰造极。牌楼，实际上是起一个门的作用，但是它的建筑形式是用牌坊形式的。按等级建造，一般有"一楼、三楼、五楼、七楼、九楼"等。

注解 9：獬豸，古代传说中的异兽，能辨曲直，见人争斗就会用角去顶坏人。

注解 10：倒插门古代的门旁边都有个插栓，锁门用的，现在倒过来了，是外面人的来开的，这是一件会被人笑的事，笑这个做门的师傅技术太差。后来形容结婚习俗。指男方入赘到女方家里，结婚后男子到女方家里落户，并且女方提供住房，吃穿等待遇。

注解 11：《陪都纪略》，同治十二年，奉天（沈阳）刘世英所著《陪都纪略》，对研究沈阳的历史文化有很大价值，书中内容广博，对杂技和宫廷舞蹈等都有记载。

注解 12：犼，读 hǒu。俗称为望天吼，朝天吼，古书上说的一种似狗而吃人的北方野兽，龙的九子之一。华表柱顶的朝天吼对天咆哮，被视为上传天意，下达民情。

注解 13：天聋地哑，主掌文运的文昌帝君身边的两个侍童，一个掌管文人录运簿册，一个手持文昌大印。道是：能知者不能言，能言者不能知。

注解 14：后人总结了昭陵十处美景，分别为"隆山积雪"、"宝鼎凝晖"、"山门灯火"、"碑楼月光"、"柞林烟雨"、"浑河潮流"、"草甸莺蝉"、"城楼燕雀"、"华表升仙"、"龙头瀑布"。

NOTES

Note 1: "Taihu Lake Three White" refers to the delicious food of carinicauda, protosalanx, whitefish produced in Taihu Lake, the second biggest lake of fresh water in China.

Note 2: This phrase is from "Yung Yey" of Analects of Confucius, "The wise take pleasures in streams; the benevolent find pleasures in hills. The wise are active; the benevolent are tranquil. The wise are joyful; the benevolent are long-lived." The wise are logical and good at dealing with affairs, like water flowing without obstacles, so the wise take pleasures in streams. The benevolent have firm faith in righteousness, which is as still as hills, and nothing can change it, therefore the benevolent find pleasure in hills. Some employ "Five Elements" theory to interpret it, according to which, "The wise possess the characteristic of earth, so they can take pleasures from water; the benevolent possess the characteristic of wood, so they can find pleasures from hills." The controversial pronunciations of three Chinese character "乐" in Confucius' words also poses questions for a long time. It is certain that pronunciations of the first two are same, but some think they are pronounced as "yao", others say they are pronounced as "yue." The third one is pronounced as "le" as in Modern Chinese, which delivers its basic meaning.

Note 3: Huangdi Mausoleum: also Mausoleum of Emperor Yellow, whose name is Xuanyuan, founder of Chinese Nation. According to folk stories, Huangdi has ascended into Heaven because of his noble virtues, so his mausoleum is a cenotaph. It stands at top of Mount Qiao, north of Huangling County in Shaan'xi Province. In 1961, the State Council designated the mausoleum to be one of the earliest key historical sites under state protection, numbering it the "No. 1 Ancient Tomb," which therefore is also titled as "The No. 1 Mausoleum."

Yandi Mausoleum: There are three altogether, including "Yandi Mausoleum of Yanling County in Hunan Province," "Yandi Mausoleum of Baoji City in Shaan'xi Province" and "Yandi Mausoleum of Gaoping City, Shanxi Province."

Dayu Mausoleum: It stands outside a temple gate of Mount Ji, three kilometers away from Shaoxing City. It is a large-scale classical building complex, which is made up of tombs, ancestral hall and temple. It covers more than 40 mu (a traditional unit of area, equaling to 0.0667 hectare or 1/6 acre), with the building area more than 2,700 square meters, It has been listed as a key historical site under state protection.

Shaohao Mausoleum: Shaohao, son of Huangdi, founded a capital city in Qiongsang, and afterwards moved to Qufu. He reigned there for 84 years, died at age one hundred years, and was buried at Shouqiu, east of the ancient capital of Lu Kingdom, which is at the northeast of Jiuxian village, four kilometers away from Qufu City. The mausoleum is 28.5 meters wide and 8.73 meters high, with its peak 12 meters high. With the shape of a pyramid, it is called as "Pyramid of China."

Qin Shihuang Mausoleum: Qin Shihuang is the first emperor of Qin Dynasty, among which "shi" means "begin" or "the first", and "huang" means "emperor." It stands at foot of Mount Li, to the east of Lintong County, which is over 30 kilometers away from Xi'an City. According to historical records, Qin Shihuang began to build his mausoleum since he came to the throne when he was 13 years old. The mausoleum was designed by his Prime Minister Li Si, and its construction was supervised by his General Zhang Han. The construction of the building lasted 38 years. This great project of grandeur has led to the fashion of lavish funerals among Chinese feudal rulers.

Han Wudi Mausoleum: Han Wudi refers to Emperor Wu of Han Dynasty, whose name is Liu Che. He is a feudal monarch with resourcefulness comparable to Qinshihuang. His mausoleum stands at Maoling Village, northeast of Xingping City (original Xingping County), which is 40 kilometers to the northwest of Xi'an City. The construction lasted 53 years from 139 B.C. to 87 B.C. It is now a key historical site under state protection.

Guangwudi Mausoleum: It is built for Eastern Han Dynasty Emperor Liuxiu (6 B.C. – 57 A.D.), courtesy named Wenshu, born in Caiyang of Nanyang (southwest of Zaoyang in Hubei Province today), the ninth grandson of Emperor Gaozu. The mausoleum was also called as Liuxiu Tomb, and it stands around Tiexie Village of Mengjin County in Henan Province. It has Mount Mang at its back and faces the Yellow River to the north. It is a big grave mound, 1400 meters in perimeter and 20 meters high. More than one thousand ancient cypresses grow here, tall and sturdy, shady and quiet.

Tang Taizong Mausoleum: Tang Taizong, Emperor Taizong of Tang Dynasty, whose name is Li Shimin, is the second emperor in Tang Dynasty. His mausoleum is called Zhaoling Imperial Tomb, the same as that of Emperor Hong Taiji, founder of Qing Dynasty. Tang-Zhaoling Imperial Tomb is the largest mausoleum among "Eighteen Mausoleums of Tang" in central Shaan'xi Plain of Shaan'xi Province, which stands on Mount Jiuzong, 22.5 kilometer to the northeast of Liquan County in Shaan'xi province.

Tang Gaozong and Wu Zetian Mausoleum: Wu Zetian is the only empress in China's history, also the oldest one that came to the throne (67 years old) and the longest living of all emperors (82 years old). She had been the empress of Tang Ggaozong (Emperor Gaozong of Tang Dynasty), and Queen Mother in the periods of Tang Zhongzong (Emperor Zhongzong of Tang Dynasty) and Tang Ruizong(Emperor Ruizong of Tang Dynasty). Later she titled herself as Emperor Wuzhou, changed Tang into Zhou, and moved her capital to Luoyang. Her monarch is historically called "Wuzhou" or "Nanzhou." She gave up the throne in 705 A.D. After she died, she requested to be buried with Tang Gaozong. Her mausoleum lies in Qian County of Xi'an, therefore also called Qian Mausoleum. It is the only mausoleum in the world that accommodates two emperors of two dynasties who were a couple. It was built in 684 A.D. and took 23 years to be completed.

Song Taizu, Zhaokuangyin Mausoleum: Zhao Kuangyin (927 – 976), first emperor of Song Dynasty, was born in Zhuozhou (Zhuo County of Hebei Province today). He had held the posts of Head Detective Inspector of Later Zhou Dynasty and military governor of Songzhou. In 960 A.D., he took the throne by starting a military mutiny at Chenqiao. Then, he changed the nation's title to Song, founded Song Dynasty, and set his capital in Kaifeng, Henan Province. He died in 976, and was buried in Mausoleum Area of Song. His mausoleum is named as Yong Chang.

Song Shenzong, Zhao Xu's Mausoleum: Zhao Xu, Emperor Shenzong of Song Dynasty, was "studious and inquisitive, forgetting to eat late in a day." When he was a prince, he liked reading military works of Han Feizi. His reigning period is from 1067 to 1085. After he died, he was buried in Yongyu Mausoleum, which was built in 1085. The stone carvings of his mausoleum are the representative works during the late period of Song mausoleums. Its modeling of stone lion and carving craftsmanship rank first among all the carvings in Song mausoleums. It is commented, "Dongling's lion, Xiling's elephant, Good stone ship in the river of Hutuo."

Song Zhezong, Zhaoxu Mausoleum: Zhao Xu (1076-1100), Song Zhezong, the 6th son of Emperor Shenzong, the 7th emperor of Northern Song Dynasty, whose original name is Yong, had been entitled King of Yan'an. Yongtai Mausoleum lies in the south of Baling Village of Zhitian Town in Gong County, four miles away from Zhitian in the northeastern direction. 400 meters away from Yongyu Mausoleum. Yongyu Mausoleum has been destroyed many times by Jin Dynasty, the cruelest of which is Song Zhezong's skeleton was strewn randomly out of the Mausoleum. Later his subordinates collected the bones, wrapped them up and placed it back again. Now there is only one earthen mound left.

Genghis Khan's Mausoleum: Genghis Khan's Mausoleum lies on Prairie of Ejin Horo Banner in Erdos of Inner Mongolia, 70 kilometers away from Dongsheng District. "Secret Burial" is popular among Mongolian, therefore, nobody knows where Genghis Khan's tomb lies. The current tomb of his is only a cenotaph. After being removed many times, it finally returned to its hometown, Ejin Horo Banner from Kumbum of Huangzhong County, 185 kilometers away from Baotou in the northern direction.

Ming Xiao Mausoleum: Ming Xiao Mausoleum is located at the west of Mount Mao, and the foot of Wanzhu Hill of Dulongfu to the southern side of Mount Zhijin (also Mount Zhong) in the east of Nanjing. The founding Emperor of Ming Dynasty, Zhu Yuanzhang, was buried here with his Empress. It is one of the largest ancient emperors' mausoleums existing, which bears characteristics of Tang and Song Dynasties and other previous mausoleums, which were built upon mountains. Later by transforming rectangular tombs into circular mounds, he started a new layout of mausoleums with features of "rectangular in the front and round in the back."

Thirteen Tombs of Ming Dynasty: Here are group tombs for emperors of Ming Dynasty, which obtained the name for burying thirteen emperors. They are located in Tianshou Hill of Mount Yan inside Changping District in the northwest suburb of Beijing. From May of the 7th year of Yongle (1407) when Chang Mausoleum began to be built to Si Mausoleum was completed for the last emperor Chongzhen, 13 mausoleums had been built within a period of more than 230 years, together with 7 tombs for concubines, 1 tomb for court eunuch. Here are buried 13 emperors, 23 empresses, 2 princes, over 30 concubines, and 1 eunuch.

Note 4: Celestial burial is an ancient and special kind of burial practices kept in Tibet of China. It is a method adopted by most Tibetans, also called "Bird Totem." It has special ground to hold the celestial burial ceremony. After death, body of the dead is carried to the celestial burial ground. The corpse is then chopped and limbs broken by the celestial burial master. After that, goshawks will blot out the sky and cover up the earth to eat up the flesh. When only skeletons are left on the burial platform, the celestial burial master will mince and wad them up, and the goshawks will descend again until all the corpse is eaten up. Surrounding people will then kneel down and pray. As a burial ceremony, celestial burial is actually a social cultural phenomenon.

Note 5: Brother ethnicities, a term proposed by the writer of this book, refer to those who are highly assimilated, closely similar in such aspects as appearance, living habits to Hans.

Note 6: Site selectors of Zhaoling Imperial Tomb has always been a puzzle for lack of definite historical records. In March of the 4th ruling year of Emperor Qianlong, there was a case regarding tomb site selection of Prince Rong, from which we can learn Du Ruyu and Yang Hongliang were exempted from death penalty for their credit of selecting sites of Yong Mausoleum, Fu Mausoleum and Zhaoling Imperial Tomb.

Note 7: The sentence is quoted from "Jinxin (2)" of Mencius, which means that a wise man would make clear first by himself, and then teach others. Nowadays, some people are not clear even themselves, but they want to make others understand.

Note 8: Pailou, a kind of memorial archway, originated from Lingxing Gate. At first it was used in worshiping Heaven, and Confucius. It was widely adopted in the watchtowers of Han Dynasty, became mature in Dynasties of Tang and Song, and till Ming and Qing Dynasties, it had reached its apex. It is actually a gate in form of Memorial arch. They are built based upon one's social hierarchy, and can generally be divided into 1 cockloft, 3 cocklofts, 5 cocklofts, 7 cocklofts, 9 cocklofts and so on.

Note 9: Xiezhi, a mythical animal in ancient legends, which can tell right from wrong, and will attack the bad person with its horn when seeing people in struggle.

Note 10: "Dao Cha Men" is a Chinese phrase used to describe the poor workmanship of a door maker, who was ridiculed as he fixed outside the inside lock. Now it refers to a kind of marriage practice, in which a bridegroom is married into and lives together with his bride's family members.

Note 11: Memoirs of Shengjing: The book was written in Mukden (Shenyang) by Liu Shiying in the 12th ruling year of Emperor Tongzhi, which covers extensive fields such as acrobatics, royal dance, and is of great value for the study of history and culture of Shenyang.

Note 12: Hou (犼), is commonly referred to as "Sky Roaring Hou", a northern dog-like beast recorded in ancient books, one of nine sons of King Dragon. The roaring of Hou at the top of ornamental column is deemed as a delivery of Heaven's will as well as civilians' living conditions.

Note 13: "Heavenly Deaf and Earthly Dumb," two servants of Wenchang, God in charge of literature, of which one is responsible for literature fortune's book, the other is in charge of God's seal. That is the rule: One who knows cannot speak while the other who can speak cannot know.

Note 14: People today summarize ten beautiful sceneries for Zhaoling Imperial Tomb, which are "Snowy Mountain," "Stone Tripod in Sunlight," "Glim of Mausoleum Gate," "Stele Pavilion in Moonlight," "Oak Trees in Misty Rain," "Tide of Hun River," "Singing Warbler and Cicada of Meadow," "Brambling of Gate Tower," "Immortality of Ornamental Column" and "Waterfall from Dragon Head."

图书在版编目（CIP）数据

昭陵／赵琛著．—北京：中国建筑工业出版社，2011.10
（世界文化遗产　辽宁卷）
ISBN 978-7-112-13604-9

Ⅰ.①昭… Ⅱ.①赵… Ⅲ.①陵墓－概况－沈阳市－清前期－汉、英 Ⅳ.①K928.76

中国版本图书馆CIP数据核字（2011）第195460号

译　　者：黄　皓　李连涛

责任编辑：吴　绫
责任设计：叶延春
责任校对：陈晶晶　关　健

世界文化遗产　辽宁卷
昭　陵
WORLD HERITAGE　LIAONING VOLUME
ZHAOLING IMPERIAL TOMB

赵琛　著

*

中国建筑工业出版社出版、发行（北京西郊百万庄）
各地新华书店、建筑书店经销
北京锋尚制版有限公司制版
北京盛通印刷股份有限公司印刷

*

开本：965×1270毫米　1/16　印张：11　字数：428千字
2011年11月第一版　2011年11月第一次印刷
定价：128.00元
ISBN 978-7-112-13604-9
（21347）

版权所有　翻印必究
如有印装质量问题，可寄本社退换
（邮政编码　100037）